Father
THERAPY

ALSO BY DOREEN VIRTUE

Books/Kits/Oracle Board

10 Messages Your Angels
Want You to Know

Awaken Your Indigo Power
(with Charles Virtue)

Veggie Mama (with Jenny Ross)

Messages from the Mermaids
Coloring Book

Messages from the Unicorns
Coloring Book

Messages from the Fairies
Coloring Book

Messages from Your Angels
Coloring Book

The Courage to Be Creative

Nutrition for Intuition
(with Robert Reeves, N.D.)

Don't Let Anything Dull Your Sparkle

Earth Angel Realms

Living Pain-Free
(with Robert Reeves, N.D.)

The Big Book of Angel Tarot
(with Radleigh Valentine)

Angels of Abundance
(with Grant Virtue)

Angel Dreams (with Melissa Virtue)

Angel Astrology 101
(with Yasmin Boland)

Angel Detox (with Robert Reeves, N.D.)

Assertiveness for Earth Angels

How to Heal a Grieving Heart
(with James Van Praagh)

The Essential Doreen Virtue Collection

The Miracles of Archangel Gabriel

Mermaids 101

Flower Therapy
(with Robert Reeves, N.D.)

Mary, Queen of Angels

Saved by an Angel

The Angel Therapy® Handbook

Angel Words (with Grant Virtue)

Archangels 101

The Healing Miracles of
Archangel Raphael

The Art of Raw Living Food
(with Jenny Ross)

The Miracles of Archangel Michael

Angel Numbers 101

Solomon's Angels (a novel)

My Guardian Angel (with Amy Oscar)

Angel Blessings Candle Kit
(with Grant Virtue; includes
booklet, CD, journal, etc.)

Thank You, Angels! (children's book
with Kristina Tracy)

Healing Words from the Angels

How to Hear Your Angels

Signs from Above (with Charles Virtue)

Fairies 101

Daily Guidance from Your Angels

Divine Magic

How to Give an Angel Card Reading Kit

Angels 101

Angel Guidance Board

Crystal Therapy (with Judith Lukomski)

Connecting with Your Angels Kit
(includes booklet, CD, journal, etc.)

The Crystal Children

Archangels & Ascended Masters

Earth Angels

Messages from Your Angels

Angel Visions II

Eating in the Light
(with Becky Black, M.F.T., R.D.)

The Care and Feeding of Indigo Children

Angel Visions

Divine Prescriptions
Healing with the Angels
"I'd Change My Life If I Had More Time"
Divine Guidance
Chakra Clearing

Angel Therapy
Constant Craving A–Z
Constant Craving
The Yo-Yo Diet Syndrome
Losing Your Pounds of Pain

Audio/CD Programs

Don't Let Anything Dull Your Sparkle
(unabridged audio book)

The Healing Miracles of Archangel Raphael (unabridged audio book)

Angel Therapy Meditations

Archangels 101
(abridged audio book)

Solomon's Angels
(unabridged audio book)

Fairies 101 (abridged audio book)

Angel Medicine (available as both 1- and 2-CD sets)

Angels among Us (with Michael Toms)

Messages from Your Angels
(abridged audio book)

Past-Life Regression with the Angels

Divine Prescriptions

The Romance Angels

Connecting with Your Angels

Manifesting with the Angels

Karma Releasing

Healing Your Appetite, Healing Your Life

Healing with the Angels

Divine Guidance

Chakra Clearing

DVD Program

How to Give an Angel Card Reading

Calendar

Angel Affirmations (for each individual year)

Card Decks

Angels of Abundance Oracle Cards
(with Grant Virtue)

Butterfly Oracle Cards for Life Changes

Loving Words from Jesus

Fairy Tarot Cards
(with Radleigh Valentine)

Archangel Gabriel Oracle Cards

Angel Answers Oracle Cards
(with Radleigh Valentine)

Past Life Oracle Cards
(with Brian Weiss, M.D.)

Guardian Angel Tarot Cards
(with Radleigh Valentine)

Cherub Angel Cards for Children

Talking to Heaven Mediumship Cards
(with James Van Praagh)

Archangel Power Tarot Cards
(with Radleigh Valentine)

Flower Therapy Oracle Cards
(with Robert Reeves, N.D.)

Indigo Angel Oracle Cards
(with Charles Virtue)

Angel Dreams Oracle Cards
(with Melissa Virtue)

Mary, Queen of Angels Oracle Cards

Angel Tarot™ Cards
(with Radleigh Valentine
and Steve A. Roberts)

The Romance Angels Oracle Cards

Life Purpose Oracle Cards

Archangel Raphael Healing Oracle Cards

Archangel Michael Oracle Cards

Angel Therapy® Oracle Cards

*Magical Messages from the Fairies
Oracle Cards*

Ascended Masters Oracle Cards

*Daily Guidance from Your Angels
Oracle Cards*

Saints & Angels Oracle Cards

Magical Unicorns Oracle Cards

Goddess Guidance Oracle Cards

Archangel Oracle Cards

*Magical Mermaids and Dolphins
Oracle Cards*

Messages from Your Angels Oracle Cards

Healing with the Fairies Oracle Cards

Healing with the Angels Oracle Cards

All of the above are available at your local bookstore,
or may be ordered through:

Hay House USA: www.hayhouse.com®
Hay House Australia: www.hayhouse.com.au
Hay House UK: www.hayhouse.co.uk
Hay House South Africa: www.hayhouse.co.za
Hay House India: www.hayhouse.co.in

Doreen's website: www.AngelTherapy.com

Andrew's website: Facebook.com/AndrewKarpenkoAuthor

Father THERAPY

HOW TO HEAL YOUR FATHER ISSUES
SO YOU CAN ENJOY YOUR LIFE

DOREEN VIRTUE

AND

ANDREW KARPENKO, MSW

HAY
HOUSE

HAY HOUSE, INC.
Carlsbad, California • New York City
London • Sydney • Johannesburg
Vancouver • New Delhi

From Doreen:
To my father, William,
and my Creator, Father God.

⁕ ⁕ ⁕

From Andrew's heart:
I would like to dedicate this book to my
birth father and my stepfather, who are my
greatest teachers. I would like to acknowledge
the lineage of my Russian forefathers. Thank You,
Heavenly Father. As a seedling pushes through
the soil, so too do we push through
our torment and grow.

CONTENTS

PART III: SPIRITUAL TRANSCENDENCE

INTRODUCTION

THERE IS HOPE FOR
HEALING FATHER WOUNDS

Congratulations for having the courage to acknowledge that you have unresolved issues with your father. In fact, you have already taken a huge step toward healing by reading this page.

There are many people who have father wounds and don't quite know what to do about it. Others have begun the journey toward healing and gotten to a certain point but become stuck. We would like to applaud you for going as far as picking up a copy of this book. It means that you have recognized that you would like to move forward.

Father wounds are sometimes discussed facetiously, with comments like "She has Daddy issues!" So intuitively we can sense the impact of having this wound, and we probably sense it in others.

Here are signs that you may have unhealed father wounds:

- Low self-esteem and lack of self-confidence

- A tendency toward people-pleasing, approval seeking, neediness, and co-dependency

- Finding yourself often wishing and praying for your dad to change into the father you believe he should be

- Frequent bouts of anger, including repressed anger

- Difficulty making your own decisions, and the desire for others to make them for you

- Choosing romantic partners who remind you of your dad or being attracted to older men
- Never feeling loved or appreciated by the men in your life
- Distrust of men
- Feeling intimidated by male authority figures
- Discomfort with religious patriarchy, such as calling God *Father* or connecting with Jesus
- Feeling like you were cheated out of the childhood you deserved
- Perfectionism (trying to be the "perfect" student, daughter, wife, employee, and so on)
- Feeling like there's an emptiness within you that you can't seem to fill
- Numbing feelings with addictions
- Sexuality issues

The more of these issues you relate to, the more your father wounds may be blocking your health, happiness, career, and relationships. *Fortunately, having an awareness of these issues is the important first step toward healing.*

Healing your father wounds frees you from feelings of emptiness, neediness, and desperation for approval and love from men. Yet the healing journey requires patience, like peeling layers from an onion. Please have faith that this process is worth the emotions you'll feel along the way—because it *is!*

Father wounds can undermine your relationships with men. The moment a man reminds you of your father, your emotional triggers revert you into a small, powerless child. You give your power away to the man in an effort to win his affection or approval. You act in ways that bring about shame . . . and the cycle continues.

Sometimes, your reaction to men could involve anger—even blind rage. You're so angry about what your father did that you superimpose him onto every man you meet. This anger pushes men away and creates a distorted viewpoint.

When you're afraid of, or angry with, your father, you may also disconnect from God the Creator. While God holds both maternal and paternal qualities, it's traditional to think of God with the male pronoun *He*. Those with father wounds often opt for gender-neutral terms such as *Source, Universe,* or *Creator*.

Additionally, father wounds can push you away from developing a close relationship with Jesus, whom we both see as a much-needed healing companion. We don't espouse the guilt-based view of Jesus, but we definitely recommend developing a loving *personal* relationship with him.

If you've had painful experiences with organized religion, we understand. Yet it's illogical to distance yourself from God and Jesus because of the people in religion. Spirituality is a human need, which can be fulfilled by your heart being open to receiving the purest healing energy imaginable.

By facing father wounds, you're able to feel the pure and unconditional love of God, Jesus, and men who are healthy and openhearted. If you crave a truly intimate and functional relationship with a man, then you have additional incentives for taking this journey of healing with us.

One important note before you read further: If you are a father yourself, you will see aspects of your fathering in this book. If this triggers guilt or regret, keep reading so that you can release and heal these issues. No one is a "perfect father," and there's always room to learn and grow, practicing new parenting skills that you'll undoubtedly receive from this book.

Although this book is written predominantly for women, it was co-authored by a gay male. I (Andrew) will discuss the impact of father wounds on my life, as well as on other men and boys. If you are a male reading this, you will find that you can relate to much of what is discussed in the book. It will also help you to understand women in your life who may be struggling with these issues.

The impact of father wounds on men and women is similar, and the healing methods used are applicable to both. The techniques are suitable for teenagers, also. Please talk to a counselor or therapist who specializes in trauma-related issues for further support.

For the men reading this book, I hope it supports your quest to heal from your father wound. The world needs more men who are in the process of healing to help bring up the next generation of healthy, balanced, loving children.

FROM DOREEN

My father is a kind and highly intellectual man. He was raised by his mother—who divorced his father when he was a small child—and aunts. So he had no father figure, and since he was an only child surrounded by powerful women, he wasn't sure what the role of a man was. He told me that he figured men weren't necessary, so he became a quiet, shy introvert.

Growing up as a sensitive young girl, I mistook my father's introversion for disapproval. When Dad was quiet, I'd often think he was upset with me. This pattern continued with my other male relationships through adulthood. And since men are prone to quietly be alone with their thoughts, I frequently felt unloved and pushed away in my relationships.

My father didn't know how to express his love verbally, like a lot of men in his generation (he was born in the 1930s). To Dad and countless other men, a father showed love by bringing home a paycheck. There were no hugs or "I love you's" from him; all nurturing was provided by my mother, who is, fortunately, very warm and cuddly.

As an adult, I became a psychotherapist specializing in treating eating disorders and addictions. They say that people become therapists to better understand themselves, and that's probably true.

Although I hadn't been abused by my father, I realized during my college training that I'd suffered from his emotional absence. Dad was always home physically, but he was absent emotionally.

So when I became a practicing psychotherapist, I had compassion for my clients' father issues. Yet I was initially unprepared for the forms of abuse they described to me. Because my clinical specialty of eating disorders involves a distorted body image, my practice was filled with women who'd been sexually abused by their fathers.

I went on to complete my Ph.D. in counseling psychology, where my doctoral dissertation was on the topic of the correlation between child abuse and the development of an addiction. That process led me through medical and psychological research about how we twist ourselves in dysfunctional ways to try to win Dad's love and approval.

My clients who'd been sexually abused had layers of anger, guilt, and sorrow that we worked upon healing together. They were angry with their abuser, with the silent parent who didn't intervene to protect them, and often with themselves. In this book, we will address many of these issues. (I've also discussed them in depth in my book *Losing Your Pounds of Pain*, which was based upon my doctoral dissertation and clinical research.)

After nearly losing my life in 1995 during an armed carjacking incident, I devoted my healing practice to God and began blending psychotherapy with spiritual counseling. I did not renew my psychotherapy registration with the state board to avoid any questions about mixing this licensure with spirituality. Although I was no longer a practicing psychotherapist, all those years of treating clients who'd been abused and abandoned by their fathers became the basis of my understanding of how to heal my own and others' father wounds.

Several years ago, I received a "Divine assignment" while I was praying and meditating. I felt Divinely guided to co-write this book with Andrew Karpenko. I'd known Andrew through my spirituality work and had been impressed by his compassionate writing style. I later found out that Andrew held a master's degree in social work— so, like me, he holds both clinical and spiritual viewpoints about healing father wounds. The result of our collaboration is the book you hold in your hands.

FROM ANDREW

When Doreen first approached me to write a book about father issues, I was a little apprehensive. I was scared of delving back into this core wound. I trust Doreen's guidance, though, and know that she is able to see deep into someone's heart and soul. She knew intuitively that I had father issues.

If you are reading this book, it is likely that you know at some level that father wounds are having an impact on your life. Maybe you are like me. I have undergone spiritual healing. I have been to kinesiologists to help with emotional issues. I have done tapping, had past-life readings, and consulted psychics and astrologers. I have prayed and I have vented. Still, time and again I came up against the same relationship issues, unhealthy eating patterns, and addictive behavior. All of the methods I tried, practitioners I visited, and workshops I attended definitely helped, and they played their part in changing patterns and beliefs and calming my traumatized nervous system.

Perhaps the missing piece in your healing is facing and feeling the pain of the past. So kudos to you for picking up this book. If I thought there was a magical affirmation, crystal, or angel that could bypass this temporary discomfort, I would have found it! Please don't get me wrong: Angels, crystals, and affirmations *can* help you heal. They are tools that I utilize regularly. I'm not advocating wallowing in pain and misery, either. I'm certainly not reinforcing a victim status. What I *am* saying is that we can embrace and balance our fears, anger, and sadness along with our love and joy.

In many ways my life is incredibly blessed. There was always food on the table. Although my parents divorced when I was about seven years old, my birth father and my stepfather helped my sisters and me by providing all the material support that we needed. I want to respectfully thank them both for everything they did for me, including helping me obtain employment.

Yet I grew up with a stepfather who was very critical and put me down a lot of the time. He was at times verbally cruel. I actually felt that he was trying to crush my spirit. He probably had narcissistic traits, and he presented himself differently to people outside of the family. All of the crueler interactions took place with no one else present. My upbringing was all about maintaining a happy, successful blended-family facade. My truth and experience was different. There were many tears and upsets. I actually blocked out many of the cruel remarks he made. In my teen years, I became rebellious. I admit my behavior was difficult. I take responsibility for my part in our interactions.

As a sensitive person, perhaps I was affected more deeply than others would have been. After all, pain and trauma are relative. Nevertheless, I believe my experiences do fit under the developmental-trauma diagnosis. (I wish to respect the privacy of living members of my family. For that reason I am not divulging their identities or the bulk of my experiences. I am sure, too, that other family members will have their own truth and perceptions. I respect them and their perspectives as well.)

My birth father was a somewhat absent father. He was around, but there was little emotional connection. I believe that he was very hurt by separating from my mother. Like Doreen's father, my father grew up in a time when men didn't express their emotions freely, and their engagement with children was more limited than today. Having a gay son who wasn't into sports was probably hard for him to deal with.

I grew up feeling like I never measured up and that I wasn't good enough because I didn't fit the stereotypical male identity. Lacking positive male role models and positive bonds with other men impacted me significantly. Without a strong sense of who I was, adolescence was a confusing time for me. I believe that this is a key component of my developing anxiety and depression around that time.

I ended up seeing a social worker in a community mental health service who helped me come to terms with my sexuality and process a lot of my family issues. My life came full circle about ten years later when *I* became a social worker and worked with teenagers, many of them involved with the corrections and juvenile justice systems.

I have worked in clinical areas of mental health, including with women, men, and children, since 2001. As a social worker, I explore each person's family system, looking at the possible impact of absent or abusive parents. I have found that father wounds are correlated with trauma and developmental issues. Conditions such as anxiety, depression, schizophrenia, and bipolar disorder can be exacerbated by the trauma of an abusive father.

Having an absent or abusive father can lead to low self-worth, self-harming behaviors, and even suicidal ideation. Some young women unconsciously seeking an abusive or absent father's love get involved with inappropriately older men. Substance abuse is also associated with father wounds.

It appears to me that this issue remains somewhat in the shadows of our psyche and is almost taboo to talk about. I've heard men in therapy groups talk about how they missed out on having positive relationships with their fathers. Yet it's not a topic of everyday discussion.

Likewise, when I approached a lot of spiritually aware women asking if they would like to submit stories for this book, often their faces would change and they would appear unsure, almost fearful, of this topic. They acknowledged that it was an issue and that they were "still working on that one!" I wish to thank the women who submitted their stories on healing father wounds. I have used several of these with their permission, de-identified to protect privacy. I also wish to acknowledge the women in my life, past and present, who have informed some of the examples used in the book.

⊗ ⊗ ⊗

The reality is that many of us are still working on our father issues. That includes the two of us. Yet we can see encouraging evidence of our healing process. For instance, I (Doreen) am no longer intimidated by male authority figures, and silent or angry men don't trigger me like they once did.

HOW TO APPROACH THIS BOOK

Our intention in these pages is to:

- Empower you so that you can deal with men as a healthy, functioning adult without being haunted by emotional ghosts from your past

- Help you choose appropriate male partners who are emotionally available and trustworthy

- Open your heart to feeling safe receiving love in an appropriate relationship

- Reconnect you with *both* Divine Feminine and Masculine spirituality

This book is intended as an exploration of father wounds. It presents a range of self-healing techniques. It is not intended as a substitute for psychotherapy, although some of the techniques could be used in conjunction with a therapist. If you are experiencing mental health concerns, we suggest seeking out professional help.

We also suggest that you be extra gentle with yourself as you read this book. Please remember to nurture yourself and take good care of yourself as you are going through it. Call upon trusted friends and health professionals, as well as prayer, for support.

FATHER THERAPY AND DIVINE TIMING

We believe that healing occurs with Divine timing. If you are reading this book, it is likely that this is the right time for you to be doing some healing. Please don't try to be perfect at doing the techniques or expect to heal everything at once. For most people, the healing occurs in stages. So you may find that you feel drawn to do one aspect of healing your father issues at a time, such as writing a letter to your father or communicating with your inner child. These can be significant pieces of work and it is suggested that you be in a reasonably peaceful place in your life when you start. Sometimes you will feel that you are making great progress and feel emotionally lighter and more whole. At other times, you might find yourself in a low place, and you may feel that you are stalled or even worry that you backslid.

It is quite normal to feel this way. Often when you are doing emotional healing, there can be periods of time when it appears that nothing is happening and you feel that you are on a plateau. That is normal as well. Often there is much going on "behind the scenes." The heart, mind, and soul are designed to heal, and they heal in a way that is safe and at a pace that we can handle.

If you feel that this book is bringing up too much to deal with at any time, feel free to put it aside until you are feeling strong enough to delve into certain topics. Try deep breathing, prayer, or playing relaxing music if you find yourself distressed. This book contains some self-soothing techniques that can be useful as well.

Don't be surprised if your father contacts you personally or you come across some correspondence from him while reading this book. It's part of the healing process. We believe that life goes on after death, so if your father has passed, it is not too late to heal that relationship. You will be helping his soul as well as your own.

You may also notice more synchronicities, such as finding other people who can support your journey. The right healing modality or healing practitioner tends to show up at the right time. Picking up this book is the first step and, through the law of attraction, has a way of connecting you with the right people, healing modalities, or other resources that will facilitate your healing of father wounds.

All your painful experiences can bring you blessings of strength, compassion, and perseverance. There are parts of your psyche calling out for healing and attention. Once you see that life is benevolent and trying to help you, your perspective changes and you can take on what seems like the daunting task of healing your father issues. Your psyche and Divine self only give you as much as you can handle at any given time.

SPREADING YOUR WINGS

The original title of this book was *The Cordelia Complex*. In Shakespeare's classic tale *King Lear*, Cordelia is the only one of the king's daughters who remains loyal to her father, yet she is misunderstood. She is banished from the kingdom because she tells him the truth. Her elder sisters placate their father and are rewarded lavishly.

If you were drawn to this book, it is likely that you too have been misunderstood and felt excluded from the rest of your family. You may, in fact, be considered a "black sheep." People who are authentic and who are true to themselves can, at times, find life more challenging. Honesty can bring conflicts. People might misunderstand your motives, and you may feel that you are pushed to the side in favor of others who say what people may want to hear.

We live in a time when it is becoming increasingly important to express our truth with compassion and love and to be true to ourselves. This can be more easily said than done. The world still seems to favor an unquestioning and passive mind, and expressing opinions that are contrary to the norm can land you in hot water.

Is this how you feel within your own family? I (Andrew) felt that way. Somehow I was different and didn't fit in with my family and with the society around me. That can lead to fear and feelings of insecurity.

Unhealed wounds from childhood and adolescence can leave you scarred. It can be as if your wings are clipped and your life hasn't taken off in the way you thought it would. Can you relate to feeling like you are limping through life, unable to reach the heights that you'd like? Are you feeling like there is more to life than the one you are living?

If this is you or you can on some level relate to this, you are not alone. We have all suffered in similar ways. The intention of this book is to allow you to break away from those old wounds and fly free! Healing this issue liberates you to pursue your passion and life purpose.

❃ ❃ ❃ ❃ ❃

A Note about Mother Wounds

If you feel that your emotional wounds also encompass your relationship with your mother, many of the healing methods outlined in this book can be of help. (We are currently working on the book *Mother Therapy* to specifically focus on this important healing work.) There are both similarities and differences between mother and father wounds. Mothers are expected to give unconditional love. While the need for paternal caring and acceptance is deep-seated, the cultural norm for fathers is to be more conditional in their love. Wounds related to either parental figure form when these needs and expectations aren't fulfilled.

Mother wounds can be particularly painful. What if the person who gave birth to us gave us away or abused, abandoned, or betrayed us? How can we move past such pain? Our healing prayers and compassion are with you, and we encourage you to adapt the techniques in this book to address those wounds.

PART I

UNDERSTANDING
FATHER WOUNDS

Chapter One

EXPLORING THE
FATHER WOUND

Primal relationships such as those that we have with our mothers and fathers run very deep, and consequently the wounding can be equally deep. The work of healing what may be profound psychological damage may in fact never be over. However, it does get easier as we melt through layers of anger and hurt. After facing these troublesome emotions, we feel like a weight has rolled off us.

If you felt shunned by your father or abandoned, ignored, abused, or betrayed, those feelings can sit within you and form a wound. Left unexpressed, they can fester, like a boil or a sore that needs to be drained. They can work away in the background without your being consciously aware of them, influencing every aspect of your life, including how you view and engage with authority figures and your intimate partners, your sense of power or self-efficacy, and your ability to create the future you want.

What makes a father's behavior wounding, to some extent, depends upon the child who was exposed to it. Children respond differently to parental behavior, and it is acknowledged that what is traumatic to one can be less so to another. It does depend upon the child's worldview and how their sense of safety and security may have been breached. Trauma can occur when an event or an absence of care leaves a child with their core identity violated or negatively altered.

The following list may trigger some memories and intense feelings of recognition. Please keep going and hang in there, because we are here to present solutions for you. But first, it's important to understand the basis for father wounds. If you need to get up and walk away from this chapter, please do take care of yourself, and then come back and read some more. You can also reach out for compassionate support while uncovering memories of childhood experiences.

Here's a helpful prayer to support your process:

"Dear God, You are my true Father Who has always been there for me. Please help me better understand my birth father and father figures, for the purpose of empowering me and healing my relationships and my mental and physical health."

TYPES OF FATHER WOUNDS

Here are some of the most common ways in which a father can wound his child. It is true that in a lot of cases, the wounding may have been unintended; however, the psychological impacts can last a lifetime unless they are acknowledged.

The Absent Father

The absent father is particularly prevalent in our society. There are several forms this absence can take. A father may be:

- **Absent part-time after a divorce or separation.**
  The child may see him only on weekends, holidays, and the like.

- **Inconsistently absent after a divorce or separation.** The child might see him at irregular and unpredictable times. This category includes a father who breaks promises to see his child or who is blocked from having contact by the mother.

- **Completely absent following divorce or other circumstances.** He or the mother moves away and severs all contact. The child never sees or knows their father. Or it may be that the mother isn't aware who the father is, including the sad situation of pregnancy by rape. In addition, imprisoned fathers may fall in this tragic category.

- **Absent due to substance abuse.** This is the father who leaves during a binge with drugs or alcohol. The family has no idea where he is, how long he'll be gone, or if he's been hurt or killed. This type of absence is abusive and leads to anxiety within the entire family.

- **Absent after passing away.** The child needs to have support to grieve and understand their father's passing. This situation is even more traumatic if violence or suicide is involved.

- **Absent because of career demands.** When a father is in the military, works in a faraway location, is touring with a sports team or musical band, or is constantly at the office, the child suffers from lack of involvement and nurturing on his part. Consistent video calls can help the child know they are being thought of and are loved.

- **Emotionally absent.** This is the father who is physically present but provides no nurturing, love, or praise to the child. This category also includes fathers who convey that the child was unwanted, or who express resentment at the expense of having children. If the child doesn't feel that they are a priority to their father, they may struggle with feelings of unworthiness and undeservingness. Fathers are often emotionally absent because of substance abuse, unhealed father wounds (or mother wounds) of their own, untreated post-traumatic stress disorder, or mental illness.

- **Financially absent.** This is the father who won't provide financial support for his child. In extreme cases, the child is left alone without food or other provisions.

All these situations create father wounds in need of healing work. The first step is admitting that this happened to you. In some families, the father's absence is never discussed. Or if it is discussed, it's done so in ways that aren't therapeutic or comforting for the children. The mother may speak of the father with angry, disparaging words, which the child may internalize. Some children believe that there is something wrong with *them* if their father is described as being so awful. Or the child may blame themselves for the father leaving.

Many children grow up not knowing who their father was. They may feel unloved and unworthy because their dad wasn't there.

Perhaps your father actually abandoned you and your family and started another family. This situation brings up fear and can set up a pattern of feeling betrayed and left behind. If a father still has contact with his first family and provides emotional and physical support with regular visits and phone calls, the impact of his absence is lessened.

In the case of the father who perhaps is physically present but emotionally absent, he may be away for work a lot or may lock himself away in an office or garage, giving the appearance of not caring and being unavailable. This pattern was prevalent for the generation who grew up in the '60s and '70s, when the men were conditioned to be physical providers only and left the child nurturing to the mother and other women in the family. The importance of a strong, loving bond with the father was less recognized back then.

Whether your father is physically or emotionally absent, the effect is the same. As a child who doesn't understand the psychology of an adult male, you may believe that you are at fault in some way—that you have done something wrong or that you somehow caused your father to be unavailable. This, unfortunately, is a recurrent pattern in children, who internalize what has happened to them, lacking the skills or the capacity to understand the adult world.

Similarly, you as a child may believe that you can win your father's love and attention through your achievements. This belief is reinforced if he gives praise only when you accomplish something, such as winning an award or bringing home A's on the report card. This can lead you to become a compulsive overachiever and a workaholic.

As an adult, you may find yourself being overly solicitous in relationships and taking ownership for issues that are your partner's responsibility. You believe it's up to you to make people happy, and if they're sad, it must be your fault. You may be convinced that you are coming from a place of love when, in fact, it is dysfunctional and can lead to co-dependency.

Here's a prayer if you grew up with an absent father:

"Dear God, please help me to feel Your healthy paternal nurturing and to know that You are my true Father, Who loves me unconditionally and completely. Please send Your angels to wrap their arms around me and allow me to feel loved."

The Addicted Father

Fathers who have active addictions, and who are not in recovery, can be wounding. They can create a chaotic family life that's very unsettling for children, who need security and routine in order to develop and feel safe.

There are different forms of addicted fathers:

- The *current substance abuser*, whose addictive behaviors are causing problems for the family, such as lost income, legal troubles, and dislocation due to an inability to maintain a job or housing. Additionally, the addict often has a volatile temper, exhibits moodiness, and may act out in abusive or abandoning ways. Some addicted fathers drag their children into bars, pubs, parties, and other inappropriate situations.

- The *past substance abuser*, who hasn't healed the underlying issues that triggered the addiction. This is known in Alcoholics Anonymous as a "dry drunk." This means a person who is no longer getting drunk or stoned but hasn't addressed what initially drove them to substance abuse.

- The *social substance abuser*, who "only" abuses drugs or alcohol during holidays or social situations. He doesn't believe there's a problem because he maintains his job and other responsibilities. Yet he is in denial that his occasional substance binges create emotional pain in his family.

- The *enabler* or *co-dependent father*, who isn't himself addicted but who enables the mother's alcoholism or substance abuse by making excuses for her.

Growing up in a tumultuous environment where you felt that life was "out of control" may have left you with a sense that the world is an unsafe place, and there is no security to be found anywhere. This can cause *insecure attachment* or *disorganized* or *chaotic attachment*, which means that you sometimes feel loving toward your father and other times you feel angry or are met with anger by your father, who is intoxicated.

This chaotic relationship with your father can lead to insecurities, anger, addiction, and relationship issues in your future.

Fortunately, as an adult you can regain more control of your life and emotions and "reparent" yourself toward better mental and emotional health.

Addictions can take on many different forms, such as compulsive gambling, alcohol and drug abuse, workaholism, and other behaviors that rob your father of his power, self-esteem, and well-being. Addicted fathers may spend their time and money on feeding their *addiction*, not their children.

Perhaps you were physically neglected, where you may have not had enough to eat or were sent to school without food or money for lunch. You may have had to wear secondhand clothes and have been laughed at and ostracized at school.

This type of neglect or poverty can leave you with a sense that your needs don't matter or cannot be easily fulfilled. You may have a pervasive sense of lack and shame that can be carried into your adult life, where you repeat the pattern of poverty.

If your father shared his alcohol or drugs with you and you got intoxicated with him when you were a child, this is especially abusive. He risked harming your developmental patterns and introduced you to an illegal situation.

Knowing this can help you to understand yourself, as well as see that this wasn't your fault. You were a child. On the other hand, blaming your parent for irresponsibility doesn't lead to healing. It may make you feel vindicated, but it won't bring you peace. Yet seeing *your* faultlessness is taking a step toward healing.

Here's a prayer if you grew up with an addicted father:

"Dear God, thank You for healing my heart and helping me to know healthy forms of love. Thank You for giving me the strength and perseverance to break the cycle of addiction in the family, beginning with myself. Please help me acknowledge, and feel safe with, my honest emotions, using healthy self-care to process how I feel."

The Abusive Father

Abusive is a loaded term that needs explaining. It can be defined as causing harm physically, psychologically, and/or emotionally.

Violent and abusive fathers are misusing their power. They prey upon vulnerable children and violate their sense of trust. In some cases, the fathers are victims of abuse themselves and are perpetuating the cycle.

Different forms of abuse include:

- **Physical abuse:** Hurting the child physically. This is never justified, nor is it legal in most cases.

- **Sexual abuse:** Taking advantage of a child, including promising gifts, love, approval, and so forth, in exchange for sexuality, and threatening the child with dire consequences if they reveal the situation to others.

- **Verbal abuse:** Calling the child names, being overly critical, or expressing doubt about the child's intelligence or abilities; threatening the child; or discussing topics a child isn't emotionally mature enough to understand or handle.

- **Psychological abuse:** Playing mind games with a child, including using guilt, fear, and anger to manipulate them.

Some studies show that psychological abuse can be just as destructive as physical abuse, if not more so. Child-safety services are now recognizing and charging people who abuse children through constant derogatory comments, manipulation, and put-downs. This type of verbal aggression can be harmful to a child's developing psyche and result in a lifetime of trauma and adjustment difficulty, including low self-esteem and addiction.

All forms of abuse can lead to post-traumatic symptoms for the child, including anxiety, sleep difficulties, addictions, relationship issues, low self-esteem, self-destructiveness, chronic anger, and flashbacks. Fortunately, these symptoms *can* be treated and healed with a commitment to facing and understanding the underlying causes.

Some abusive fathers are untreated alcoholics or addicts, and these substances and intoxication lead to abusive behavior. This is not to excuse or justify abuse, but to understand it so that the adult children of abuse can move toward healing. Some fathers have anger-management issues, and their physically or emotionally abusive behavior stems from their inability to regulate their emotions and express their needs in constructive ways. Once again, this is not an excuse for their actions, though.

Abusive fathers usually have mental health issues that need treatment. However, in the case of narcissistic fathers (those who perpetually blame others for their problems), there's a lack of motivation to change.

Fortunately, there are services available for men who are able to recognize that their behavior is destructive. If they can take responsibility for their actions and are committed to change, then change *is* possible. While this doesn't erase the past, a new, healthier openness about acknowledging abuse means that more people are coming forward, speaking up, and regaining their sense of power.

Here's a prayer if you grew up with an abusive father:

"Dear God, I need Your help, please, to see myself through the eyes of the angels, so that I can know my worth and value. Please allow me to shed the negativity and focus upon how to help others with the same experiences I've had. Thank You for supporting my process of learning how to be at peace."

THE LEGACY OF PATERNAL INFIDELITY, DIVORCE, AND RELATIONSHIP INSTABILITY

If your father cheated on your mother, you're more likely to believe that all men are unfaithful. Unfortunately, you may also attract romantic relationships with unfaithful men in an unconscious desire to change your father.

Infidelity bursts a child's bubble about having a safe and lasting family system. This is especially true if the affair results in the father moving out of the house. So the child tries to understand why their world was shattered by their father's affair. Many blame themselves in an attempt to make sense of the infidelity and divorce, which can lead to depression and anxiety, unless they receive emotional support and understanding from a caring counselor or family member.

This can also include "emotional infidelity," in which the father is physically monogamous but cheats on his wife by flirting or by watching or reading pornography. Children become confused and disheartened when they learn that their father is attracted to other women.

If the mother divorces the father because of the infidelity, the child feels grief from the loss of Dad, plus anger at the reason for his absence. In most cases of infidelity, the child's mother will be so distraught that she cannot provide emotional support.

Children thrive on parental consistency, which means the ability to predict when and where they'll next see their father and mother. In a chaotic, anger-filled divorce setting, many children have inconsistent schedules with their noncustodial parent (often the father).

In addition, the mother may tell the child horrible stories about the father. The child may conclude that if their father is "bad," they are one-half bad as well. They then may generalize that "all men are bad," and lack the trust that's necessary for them to have a long-term romantic relationship.

Unfortunately, a child's belief that all men are cheaters may result in attracting a cheating partner as an adult. This is done unconsciously, through the law of attraction.

There are many men who are faithful to their spouses, yet finding one first involves being attracted to "nice guys." A lot of women with father wounds are bored with men who are nice. They are attracted to "bad boys," like their father—a topic we will address in the next chapter, which delves deeper into the long-term impact of a fractured father relationship. Connecting the dots of how your father wounds have affected your romantic life, plus prayer, can also help you be in the healthy relationship that you desire and deserve.

⚘ ⚘ ⚘ ⚘ ⚘

Chapter Two

THE IMPACT OF FATHER WOUNDS

Girls *and* boys are impacted by the absence of a loving father figure in their lives. Research shows the influence of the father is just as important as that of the mother, and in some instances more important.

There are many benefits to having a loving father or father figure. Such children have fewer behavioral problems. Girls perform better in mathematics and are less likely to abuse drugs and alcohol. Boys, too, do better academically and are more likely to have a strong sense of who they are and treat women in the same respectful way their father did.

WOUNDED FEELINGS

Father wounds can affect you in ways you may not at first realize. For example, if your father didn't express his love to you, then you may unconsciously believe that you must not be worthy of love or that you are unlovable. It is connected to a feeling and a belief that you don't deserve good in your life. As a consequence, your life circumstances can reflect that. Your present pain may be replicating hurt that is within from the time you were a child.

You may find that you have feelings of low self-esteem. As we mentioned, feeling insecure, unloved, and not respected as a child can lead to depression and anxiety. The impact of trauma is being studied and is being linked to the development of mental health conditions.

Abusive behavior from a father figure is correlated with later addiction to alcohol or drugs and unhealthy relationships. Unhealthy behaviors can be a way of coping with uncomfortable feelings that are a result of the trauma you experienced. Alternatively, you may find yourself covering up your feelings by working too much. You may be successful in terms of your achievements, yet feel lonely and empty underneath that veneer of success.

This can lead to a hollow feeling deep inside you, especially when you are alone or trying to fall asleep at night. That feeling can be a precursor of despair. It can also be a path to compulsive behaviors such as overeating or alcohol abuse.

There is a way of overcoming and mastering these feelings. Many believe that their feelings are in control of them rather than the other way around. These feelings seem to have a life of their own. In fact, we may have experienced them for as long as we can remember, and thus we accept them as natural or normal and conclude there is nothing that we can do about it.

You are not alone—a lot of us have felt and still feel this way. The good news is that it is *never* too late to heal and to recover from trauma or feeling wounded.

Heeding Your Inner Knowing

Pain (emotional and physical) is often a signal that it is time to stop and consider what is going on in our lives. Those feelings, our interior guidance system, are a part of us that is alerting us that something is wrong and needs our attention. It is like those sensor systems in cars that ding, telling us to put our seat belts on, or that light up, telling us to check something under the hood.

An inner knowing is advising us when something is a little off and needs our attention. It can seem easier at first to ignore these warning systems and keep driving. If we disregard the softer dings, then the alarm gets louder and begins to command our attention.

Life can veer off course when you refuse to listen to the warning signals and keep on going. If in doubt, "pull over." Stop to examine what your feelings are telling you before continuing down that road.

Patterns of Pain

If you had a difficult childhood and experienced abuse, disappointment, or separation from your father or other challenging situations, it can seem as if you are caught up in an endless loop of pain.

You may feel unfulfilled, as though your relationships at work and your personal life constantly mirror the events or sensations of your painful past, including believing that:

- Your career is constantly blocked or that you continually meet dead ends.

- You lack the passion and drive to commit to your goals.

- Life is very harsh and not generous.

- You are unappreciated.

- Your opinions don't matter.

- You are being taken advantage of and mistreated.

It may be time to reflect now on any similarities between your relationship with your father and the relationships that you have with others. Specifically take notice of your relationships with other males or authority figures (male or female). They represent father energy as well.

It can be a little overwhelming to look at your past patterns and obstacles that you've experienced in your relationships and your career. Like an artist before an easel, sometimes you may need to redraw or repaint the same picture before you are ready to tackle another subject. Life reflects our painful past over and over until we learn another way and consciously heal.

For example, Gloria's father died when she was five years old. She was not able to develop a close bond with him, as she was so young when he passed away. Gloria got married when she was 18, yet she found that she didn't have an emotional connection with her husband. She later sensed that he married her for money and status and that he was emotionally disconnected in the marriage.

Gloria and her husband ended up getting separated. Gloria saw the pain of her separation as a wake-up call and an opportunity to examine and heal her life. She began a journey of self-exploration through reflection and reading self-help books. She recognized the connection between having a father who passed when she was a child and having a husband with whom she was emotionally distant.

Gloria realized that the little girl inside her was craving the love of her father. However, she had to love herself, as nobody outside her could be a substitute for her deceased dad. When Gloria realized what was happening, she was able to start a new life for herself, using her divorce as an opportunity to claim her freedom from the past. This freedom gave Gloria the space to attract a new relationship into her life. Her career also improved. She ultimately found emotional fulfillment with a loving partner and joy in a successful career.

WHAT SIGNS INDICATE THAT YOU HAVE A FATHER WOUND?

One of the primary ways in which father wounds can show up in our lives is through our relationships. The relationship that you have with your father can influence all your subsequent ones and how you approach life in general.

An Attraction to Emotionally Unavailable or Abusive Men

After we have experienced what may have been a challenging childhood or a turbulent adolescence, we go on to form adult relationships where the telltale signs of having a father wound show up, asking us to pay attention and begin the healing process.

For example, if you had a kind and loving father, you are more likely to look for a kind and loving partner. Of course, the opposite is also true. If your father was cold and distant, then you may find that you seek out partners who are similarly unable to express their emotions. It's an unconscious desire to "fix" your father and finally receive the love and approval you crave.

Women who, sadly, have abusive fathers may seek out partners who are abusive because that is a pattern they experienced when they were young. It's all they know, even though it's painful.

This happens on a subconscious level. We don't consciously go out to find someone who is cold and unemotional and who will not fulfill our emotional needs. However, until we actually stop and reflect and ask ourselves, *Why do I keep attracting men who are emotionally unavailable?* we continue the pattern.

Andrew: I have found myself in relationships where the other person was simply not emotionally available. I believe that I attracted this type of one-way relationship, in which my feelings were not often reciprocated, because of the father wound. The part of me that was looking for love and acceptance from other males was really my psyche trying to heal the father wound.

Unfortunately, coming from a place of need doesn't work, and you may keep attracting the same sort of relationship until you openly look at the pattern and examine the reasons why you keep replaying it.

In Part II of this book, you will learn how to do healing work with your inner child, and as you heal, you will begin to attract more balanced relationships. Affirmations can also help you begin new patterns of behavior.

Affirm:

*"I choose healthy relationships that rerflect my high self-worth.
I allow myself to attract a kind and loving partner."*

An Attraction to Older Men

Whether you are a heterosexual woman or a gay man, being attracted to older men can be a sign that you have father wounds or issues that you will want to look at. An older partner may be financially secure, worldly, and generous with his advice and protection. Often, though, when there is a significant age difference, the relationship is controlling or can become co-dependent in that you look to a stronger male figure to fulfill your unmet needs.

In effect, this partner is acting as a father figure within the context of an intimate relationship. In truth, this is like a father-child relationship that can, for a period of time, give you that sense of security, stability, and feeling loved that you have craved all your life. This type of relationship tends to not last long, as there is a power imbalance, and you may outgrow it as you mature and find your own sense of inner strength.

Affirm:

"I am in charge of my life. I care for and support myself."

An Attraction to the "Bad Boy" or "Man Child"

Similarly, you may have been attracted to "bad boys" who provide a lot of excitement and drama. You can be unconsciously drawn to men who aren't really emotionally stable or mature enough to be able to form healthy relationships. If you did not have a stable, loving relationship with your father, you don't have that role model to be able to replicate in your own life. As a consequence, you may choose unstable, immature, or unavailable partners.

Father wounds may have also resulted in you being attracted to a "man child." These types of men appeal to your nurturing side. Becoming a mother figure to boys who are in men's bodies can fulfill that maternal instinct. Unless the male is aware and is willing to develop his adult self, these relationships will have a mother-son dynamic. If your father wasn't mature and emotionally secure, you may be unconsciously attracted to men who are insecure, childlike, and seeking more of a mother figure than an equal partner.

In these cases, you have a need to feel needed and an unconscious desire to heal your father. So you give everything to the man child, and he takes advantage of, or doesn't appreciate, your giving nature. Usually he becomes entitled and spoiled. Nurturing yourself and nurturing your own life can be more helpful.

If you find yourself repeating these patterns, ask yourself why that is. Through self-reflection and deliberate effort, you can break these patterns and choose relationships with men who are emotionally mature and self-aware.

Affirm:

- *"I allow God and the angels to choose partners who are healthy for me."*
- *"I allow myself to meet new people who are outside of my 'type.'"*
- *"I allow romantic love to unfold in Divinely orchestrated ways."*

Feeling Insecure, Jealous, and Vulnerable

As a result of not having a stable, loving father while you were growing up, you may be prone to feeling jealous and insecure in relationships. These feelings are often covering up a sense of being vulnerable and unsafe, because that's how you felt in your childhood.

This insecurity can lead you to not trust your partners, smother them, or try to control and monitor their actions. It is as though your inner compass is constantly attuned to finding fearful situations wherever you go. Looking for reasons to worry is called *hypervigilance.*

It can be unpleasant to realize that at times, you can feel hypervigilant. These feelings are normal, and it is important to acknowledge them. Acknowledging these tendencies and understanding where they come from is a major part of healing.

This can take a while, because often the patterns are working within your subconscious mind. Bringing these beliefs and tendencies into the light of awareness means that you can let them go and begin to have a loving and trusting relationship with yourself, your partner, and life.

Affirm:

"I am in a trusting relationship with life. I feel safe, and I know that I can trust in my Higher Self, God, Jesus, and the angels."

The "Never Enough Love" Syndrome

Another way in which father issues can show up is feeling that you constantly need demonstrations of love, reassurance, and affection from people around you, particularly your partner.

Do you feel as though that inner "love bucket" is never full? Like no matter how many compliments are paid to you or how much affection you're given, it's not enough? It can seem as though that bucket has holes in the bottom of it.

We all feel needy at times. That is part of being human; however, if that need is insatiable, it can be draining on the people in our lives, including intimate partners.

We are created perfect, whole, and complete by God. Yet childhood experiences may leave us feeling *incomplete*. Your inner child, hungry for a father's love and affection, sits within your subconscious mind, begging for approval.

Acknowledging these needs can be a scary but necessary first step in addressing this "never enough love" syndrome. Once your inner child feels safe, secure, and loved, then you no longer feel the need to seek out love from everyone around you. You will be more fun to be around, and your partners and others will enjoy your company and won't find you draining.

Working on self-healing can feel tough at first. Yet it delivers rewards not only to you but to everyone around you.

Affirm:

"I nourish myself with God's love. I love and approve of myself."

Compulsively Acting Out Sexually

We may sometimes seek to fulfill our emotional needs through sex. Father wounds can affect our sexuality in one of two ways: (1) compulsively indulging in sexuality with multiple partners, or (2) avoiding sexuality completely.

Sex is something that is pleasurable for most people. However, a line can be drawn between *enjoying* and *compulsively engaging in* sex. Feeling out of control when it comes to engaging in sexual activity can signal an attempt to get your deeper emotional needs met through sex. This form of sexual behavior can be an addiction.

We all crave love and attention. That is part of who we are as human beings. It is a part of the human condition. Having lots of sex can temporarily give you a false feeling of being loved. If you continue a pattern of casual sex, you may miss out on developing relationships that are based on love, respect, and companionship.

Please don't judge yourself. This is really about being honest with yourself and discerning whether you are engaging in sexual activity out of genuine passion or due to a compulsion.

No one wants to admit that they are feeling lonely and unloved and are seeking love and intimacy through sex. Yet admitting your true feelings to yourself is an important healing step.

Studies also show that a high percentage of prostitutes (both female and male) are sexual-abuse survivors. This abuse, often perpetrated by the father or a father figure, damaged their self-esteem, and some believe their "worthiness" is tied to their sexual performances.

Sexual feelings are normal. It's how you act on them that determines whether they are healthy or dysfunctional. Is your sexuality bringing up shame? This can be a sign of needing to forgive yourself and perhaps receive some psychotherapy support. Do your sexual acts leave you feeling empty? This is a sign of the need for more emotional connection with your partner or partners. Does your sex life seem unsatisfying because it is masking other urges? This is a sign that you may need to express yourself creatively in artistic ways.

If you have been having unprotected sex or engaging in sexual relationships that are causing you or others problems, then part of your healing and self-care will be to stop entering into destructive sexual situations.

A counselor who is skilled in treating addictions can safely and compassionately help you to identify and heal these underlying issues. In addition, the free international 12-step support group Sex and Love Anonymous (which also has online meetings you can easily locate with an Internet search) can help you address the core basis of sexual and romantic addictions.

Affirm:

*"I express my sexuality from a place of love,
wholeness, and true passion. I understand the
difference between passion and compulsion."*

Sexual Dysfunction

Those who were sexually abused or raped may develop a dislike of sexuality, because it holds flashback triggers to the abuse situations. This can lead to *frigidity,* or a lack of sexual appetite. Sexual dysfunction can also appear as a phobia of being physically intimate with a partner; body dysmorphia (disliking how you look); and workaholism, where you're too busy with your career to have a romantic relationship.

Some abuse survivors become "auto-sexuals," people who only have sexual relations with themselves through fantasy and compulsive masturbation. The fear of intimacy with another person can become a phobia preventing a person from enjoying a relationship. If this person does get married, there can be misunderstandings, hurt feelings, and even affairs or divorce if the issue is left untreated.

A therapist specializing in trauma treatment is usually necessary for healing from sexual dysfunction that arose from rape or sexual abuse. Fortunately, utilizing the EMDR (Eye Movement Desensitization and Reprocessing) therapeutic method can help the healing process be gentle. You can find an EMDR-trained therapist on the EMDR Institute website. (Please see the Appendix for information on therapeutic resources.)

Affirm:

- *"I love and respect myself."*
- *"I honor myself and my body."*
- *"I treat myself with respect."*
- *"I express my sexual desire with love and creative endeavors."*

THE DRAMA LOOP

If your relationship with your father was traumatic and you feel like you don't have control of your external events and patterns, you may experience a drama loop of feeling up temporarily before your mood crashes.

Drama can be addictive. Each time an old wound is reopened or someone who mirrors our father pain comes into our lives, circuits connected to our trauma fire in our brains. As part of the trauma response, the body releases a raft of stress chemicals that are akin to taking a stimulant drug.

Some of the hormones released during stress can give us a type of buzz that lifts our mood out of the doldrums that we may be feeling. Over time, of course, this wears out our adrenal system, and all the drama and stress hormones usually don't lead to making new, healthier choices.

Being in a pattern of fight, flight, freeze, or fawn can be like an addiction. It is an endless loop of pain that can keep us stuck. We may not consciously be aware of it, however, when our work and personal lives are filled with challenging relationships. The drama and our physiological responses actually give a temporary boost in our mood. I (Doreen) have written about this topic extensively in my book *Don't Let Anything Dull Your Sparkle.*

This position of pain and drama can feel familiar and oddly "safe" because it is probably all you have ever known for most of your life. That in itself can be a painful realization, and there may be a feeling of hopelessness and powerlessness to do anything about that pain.

Some of the time you may feel like running away and avoiding everything through binge eating or alcohol and drugs. These are all temporary measures that make you feel better briefly; however, the net of pain gets tighter as you add feelings like shame, guilt, and remorse into the mix.

You're not alone in this cycle, and many people have been through the journey of addiction. If you're currently engaged in behavior that's decreasing your self-worth, health, or well-being, it's essential to examine this pattern.

FATHER PAIN AND ADDICTIONS

Have you struggled with low self-esteem and difficult emotions that have led you to addictive behavior? Both of us have had such struggles, and we realize that the behavior was a way of "medicating" our emotions. Fortunately, we each recognized this pattern so that we could deal with it effectively.

If you are overwhelmed with a sense of emptiness, loneliness, or depression, and you haven't found effective ways of managing those emotions, you can find yourself vulnerable or predisposed to addictive behavior. This involves:

- Having uncontrollable and obsessive cravings for a substance or behavior

- Feeling that you have no choice but to indulge in the substance or behavior

- Experiencing problems in your health, relationships, career, finances, education, and so forth because of the substance or behavior

- Feeling a chronic sense of guilt and shame about the behavior

Whether you turn to food, surfing the Internet, gambling, shopping, alcohol, or drugs, excessively bingeing has consequences for your health and self-esteem. These substances and activities stimulate the pleasure centers of the brain and release the feel-good neurochemicals dopamine, opioids, and serotonin that create a pleasant elation or numbing sensation.

If you either find yourself engaging in addictive behavior or believe you are hooked on pain and drama, please don't feel embarrassed or hesitate to seek support.

Doreen: I have lost two beloved people due to the consequences of addictions: my grandfather, who was killed by a drunken driver, and a dear friend, who overdosed on prescription pain medication. Addictions are not to be taken lightly or with the hope that they will "go away" on their own. Addictions rob us of happiness, health, time, respect, and money. No high or numbing experience is worth this. Brigitte Parvin, a sobriety coach, and I are co-authoring a book about addictions called *How to Get Your Life Back.*

If you are in the grips of an addiction, we recommend that you seek professional help either through phone or face-to-face counseling services. Some people need in-patient detox and residential rehabilitation programs. Others find the free 12-step support groups (such as Alcoholics Anonymous, Overeaters Anonymous, Narcotics Anonymous, Debtors Anonymous, Emotions Anonymous, or Al-Anon for co-dependency issues) helpful ways to recover from addictions. These programs, found worldwide and through online meetings, help you know that you're not alone by connecting you with others who've experienced similar processes. You have a sponsor whom you can contact outside of the group.

The first of the 12 steps is to admit your powerlessness over the addiction. This is a humbling experience that opens you to receiving support from God, a counselor, and your 12-step sponsor. Studies show that prayer and spirituality are helpful in healing from addictions. (We will discuss the power of prayer in Chapter 9.)

❊ ❊ ❊

The way that healing works for most people is a gradual process. It is the proverbial "layers of an onion" that need to be peeled back and revealed. Most of us can only deal with a little bit of the pain and discomfort at a time. Doing too much or trying to make too many changes or to heal everything at once can set you back in the long run.

Remember to forgive yourself and be gentle during this "healing time" when you are actively reading this book. The next chapter explores just how prevalent the father wound is—woven into the cultural tapestry of our myths and fables—and presents examples of healing to light your path.

❊ ❊ ❊ ❊ ❊

Chapter Three

FATHER HUNGER AND OTHER ARCHETYPAL WOUND PATTERNS

What is that deep longing that we all feel from time to time? How many of us have felt that dull ache and unfulfilled need to be loved and cherished by someone outside us? That inner *father hunger* is a craving for love, masculine energy, and approval.

HUNGER FOR LOVE

Father hunger can show up in adolescent girls and boys as truancy or dropping out of school, having many sexual experiences and partners at a young age, and teenage pregnancies. For young women and girls, early sexual behavior is a "hunger" for male love and attention. They are trying to compensate for the loss of their father's love through seeking contact with the opposite sex. Girls feel the loss of their father's love as a rejection of themselves. Unfortunately, this sense of lack and unhealthy neediness can lead girls and women to be sexually exploited by men and, in some cases, by women.

Liz's father was often busy and preoccupied and appeared to be oblivious to her needs as a little girl. He grew distant from her as a teenager. This was when she sought out the company of boys and later men.

Liz felt attracted to boys when she was in early high school. She enjoyed the attention and secretly craved love. Physical affection was what she needed the most; however, she was unable to express this need clearly or healthily.

Unfortunately, some boys and men sensed her vulnerability and exploited her need for love and affection. Liz engaged in sexual behavior as a way of meeting her emotional needs. She particularly enjoyed the physical affection that came with sex. Despite regularly seeking out this type of affection, Liz found that the inner need for love was only temporarily met, and the boys she went out with grew tired of her. She experienced the same rejection from boys that she experienced with her father.

She continued her pattern of being sexually available as a way of seeking love and affection into adulthood. Although initially Liz felt that her love hunger and father hunger needs were being met, she soon realized that she felt empty. She also felt exploited in her relationships with men. As time went by, Liz was left feeling used, and her self-esteem suffered. After counseling and doing some self-reflection, Liz was able to identify that she was trying to compensate for the love and affection she did not receive from her father.

Liz poured her heart out in a letter she wrote to her father. She expressed the sense of abandonment, loss, and rejection that left her wounded and vulnerable. Liz didn't send the letter but instead released it by burning it. She felt relieved after purging her feelings of hurt and rejection. She also released the guilt she felt over her sexual exploits.

Liz decided to take a year away from men, to discover who she was and what her real values were. She felt better about herself by taking art classes and found new female friends. Liz's wound began to heal through her newfound sense of self.

UNCOVERING SOME ARCHETYPAL WAYS
THAT FATHER WOUNDS CAN SHOW UP

The Cinderella Complex

Do you remember how enchanted you were with this popular fairy tale? Cinderella's father wasn't there to protect her, and she had to contend with a mean stepmother and stepsisters until she was delivered from their house.

Perhaps you thought that your life story would involve the "happily ever after" ending—that is, meeting the handsome prince.

Do you have a secret desire to be rescued? Are you waiting for the prince to save the day and love you?

Fairy tales and romantic movies often offer this "prince saving the maiden" story line. This sets a woman up to see men as the ones who will fix everything, and then feel disappointed when she discovers they're wounded people too.

With the Cinderella Complex, the longing for a loving father figure has been replaced by the powerful myth of a prince who takes care of you and you live happily ever after. The movie *Pretty Woman* contains some parallels to this, with Julia Roberts's character being similarly rescued. Unfortunately, life doesn't seem to work that way. Even if you do meet your "prince," you could be putting too many expectations onto the other person. In truth, no one can really fulfill all those unmet needs.

Cindy had a successful career. She took care of her appearance and had a wide circle of friends. There was one area in her life that was not working, though: her intimate relationships. She seemed to date one guy after another. Initially they got along well, but she quickly pinpointed their faults and failings. This soon led to arguments and disharmony in the relationship. What Cindy wasn't aware of was that she was looking for a man who was going to treat her like a princess to compensate for her father's neglect. She, in turn, had very high standards and unrealistic expectations about how she wanted to be treated.

At first, she couldn't see how her unmet needs from childhood were being replayed in her relationships. When her counselor pointed out this pattern, Cindy admitted that she was influenced by romantic novels and movies growing up. She had inhabited a fantasy world to escape the disappointment of a childhood without nurturing.

Cindy adjusted her expectations of her latest partner and found compromises. She was still able to inject love and romance into her relationship; however, she had more realistic expectations and a more balanced view of her partner. She also accepted his human faults and imperfections. She was able to focus on his positive aspects and strengths.

The Cinderella Complex involves an archetype similar to that of the eternal little girl or the princess who seems caught up in a perpetual childhood or adolescence. Something traumatic happened in their childhood, and a part of them remained frozen in a childlike state. Their development became stuck or "arrested" somewhere in their past.

When we are children, there is a need to depend upon others for our safety and survival. But if we never grow up, we may evade responsibility for our own lives.

If you identify with this desire to be rescued or have a male partner provide for you, then recognizing this tendency is crucial in taking steps toward maturing from this pattern. Being a fairy-tale princess sounds fabulous, yet wanting to be treated like royalty and lacking your own agency or autonomy can be disempowering and taxing to those around you.

The Superwoman

Traditionally, fathers—especially in prior generations—have maintained a role in society as breadwinners and shut themselves off from their feelings. As a consequence, many girls have not been nurtured by men. They may then model themselves after a father who didn't show his vulnerability and often wore a stoic mask.

Feeling consistently numb and unemotional may be signs that you've become a *superwoman*. This term refers to a woman who is more concerned with accomplishments and accolades than inner peace.

Men historically dominated the business world and many professions. Then the 1980s brought widespread adoption of the dress-for-success ideas and shoulder pads, and women who projected a steely facade attained positions in power. To survive in tough, male-dominated environments, women learned to stuff down their feelings and become supercompetitive. Some women lost touch with their own femininity, emotions, and vulnerability in order to cope. Drive, ambition, and achieving goals are now accepted norms and desirable traits for both men and women.

Linda grew up as a bit of a tomboy. She was close to her dad, and together they enjoyed outdoor activities and sports. Yet her father—like many from an earlier generation—was not a nurturer.

As she grew up, she noticed that she needed to behave in a competitive and masculine way to gain promotions in her nursing career. Although nursing was a female-dominated profession, she still felt compelled to display dominant behavior to get ahead. One night, Linda felt disheartened by her work culture and the sort of person she'd become in order to succeed at her career.

Linda had risen to a unit manager position when she found that her female colleagues no longer responded to her warmly. She'd allowed her ambition and drive to overtake her more nurturing qualities. After talking to some of her mentors, she realized that she could still be kind, warm, empathetic, and caring without sacrificing her power or her position. She learned that she could balance being a strong leader in her role as unit manager without losing herself and her femininity. Linda found that her staff began to respond to her warmth, and the whole energy of her work environment positively shifted.

Female superheroes, past and present, also seem to exhibit strong male characteristics. Wonder Woman, Xena, and Lara Croft of *Tomb Raider* fame are strong and sexy instead of gentle and classically feminine. While it may seem admirable to be a superwoman, this path can also be cold and lonely. And if your emotions are numb, it's impossible to feel a happy sense of accomplishment, love, or peace. Everything is about competing and winning.

In order to work effectively in business or in any career, keeping calm and being relatively unemotional is often necessary. There's a need to balance your emotions with your more rational side. Learning to balance and calm your emotions with simple techniques is discussed later in this book.

In personal relationships, being a superwoman can discourage emotional intimacy. People may admire you or be intimidated by you, but what most are looking for in a friend is someone they can feel comfortable with. You don't want to push away good friendships by being overly tough.

No one is saying that you need to be perfect or have all these issues sorted. We are all works in progress. Balancing your masculine and feminine sides is important for both men and women, and is something to work on daily. As a woman, you can be simultaneously powerful and feminine. Men can be strong, active, and driven and also be nurturing and sensitive. The traditional male identity is softening, which is great to see.

If you are a woman who works in a predominantly male industry, you may come home from work with your male energy in full force. Take some time, then, to transition into your feminine side when you arrive home—for example, changing out of your work clothes and playing some soft music, meditating, soaking in a salt bath, doing gentle yoga stretches, or talking with a heart-centered friend.

Doreen: I see Mother Mary as a wonderful role model of a woman who is both highly feminine and superbly strong. She is, of course, also nurturing and has excellent boundaries. I highly recommend working with Mother Mary through prayer and meditation to connect with her Divine balance of feminine and masculine energies. You can also visit a Marian site such as Lourdes, Guadalupe, or Fátima to gain a closer relationship with Mother Mary as your guide and mentor.

The Wounded Child

If you endured a challenging childhood with an abusive or absent father, you likely have a wounded child within you. This part of you can show up in your adult life through feelings of being powerless, not good enough, or unworthy.

Having a wounded inner child is similar to raising a child who acts out. Your inner child may throw tantrums, so as an adult you find it difficult to regulate your emotions. You may feel like you are prone to having emotional outbursts such as uncontrollable anger, immobilizing fear, and overwhelming sadness a lot of the time.

Your inner child may be trying to get the attention of your adult self by "being naughty." The child self may want to sabotage your decision-making or find other ways of misbehaving. The unhealed child may impulsively veer toward addictions and other indulgences.

Would you permit a child to drive a high-powered vehicle? That is what occurs if you allow your wounded inner child to run your life. If you suspect or know you have a wounded inner child, the first step is to give it appropriate attention. Don't hand it the keys to your life, but do listen to your feelings and reassure your inner child that you're a trustworthy adult caretaker. And then *be* that trustworthy adult caretaker by taking responsible care of yourself.

Some people find the process of dialoguing with their inner child threatening, or may not know where to start or how to access this powerful inner child. There's an outline of some processes that you can use in Part II of this book.

How would you treat a child who was hurting and sad? You would comfort them and treat them with love and compassion, and you would want to take them in your arms and embrace them. Instead, we have a tendency to ignore, suppress, or chastise that part of us that urgently needs love and attention. Too often, we view asking for love as weakness instead of a sign of strength. Tragically, when the wounded inner child is ignored, it "screams" louder by acting out or through body ailments.

A wounded inner child can be a powerful ally and a great teacher. After you have worked with and integrated that aspect of yourself, you will find that feelings of self-compassion, self-understanding, and self-acceptance emerge.

❉ ❉ ❉

There are, of course, many other ways in which your father wound can show up. This can include a fear of being abandoned and having trust issues. Healing these fears and working on developing a trusting relationship with yourself are discussed in Part II of this book.

Please understand that we know these are broad headings and labels. In truth we are all complex beings, and none of us are going to fit neatly into these categories. They are meant to be a guide only. As we have said before, recognizing patterns that recur in your life is the first step toward healing them.

THE SHADOW FATHER IN FAIRY TALES, MYTHOLOGY, AND MOVIES

Your story of your troubled relationship is not unique and has been played out throughout history. The purpose of explaining this is not to minimize your pain or to diminish your experience. It is, however, designed to show you that other people have gone before you and have overcome their issues with their fathers. The father wound has been mythologized since ancient times, recognized as an archetypal pattern within the human experience.

Fairy tales, myths, the Bible, literature, and movies have told the story of relationships between fathers and daughters and fathers and sons. More often than not, these stories have been filled with conflict, misunderstanding, and even death.

Classic Greek mythology features the story of Oedipus, who killed his father after falling in love with his mother. This myth was used by Sigmund Freud in psychoanalysis to explain tensions between fathers and sons, as well as fathers and daughters.

Modern-day stories, soap operas, and plays continue to tell of the impact of the absent father.

Absent and passed-on fathers are a constant theme in fairy tales and movies. A recent survey of Disney and Pixar children's films found that 40 out of 69 characters were portrayed with a deceased, missing, or single parent. Peter Pan, of course, lacked parental figures, and Jasmine (*Aladdin*), Belle (*Beauty and the Beast*), and Pocahontas are characters raised by a single father. (This may have been because of the tragic death of Walt Disney's mother, who passed away because of a gas leak in a house that he'd purchased for her.)

Examining traditional fairy tales reveals an archetype called the *shadow father.* The way in which fathers are represented is surprisingly negative.

Take the example of Cinderella, whose mother died and whose father remarried a wicked stepmother with two wicked stepsisters who tormented her. According to the classic rendition of the fairy tale, Cinderella could not go to her father for help: "The poor girl bore it all patiently, and dared not tell her father, who would have scolded her; for his wife governed him entirely."[1]

Cinderella's father then leaves the family home and is killed, and the stepmother inherits the house—and her stepdaughter. Cinderella's life takes a horrible turn with her father's death, and hope is renewed only when she marries a prince. "Cinderella" is overall a heroic story in which, despite the odds being stacked against her, the heroine does find her prince and has the fairy-tale ending of "happily ever after."

If only life worked that way. We don't subscribe to the myth of happily ever after because life does throw us challenges. On the other hand, you *can* overcome an oppressive childhood and live the life of your dreams, which does come close to the "happily ever after" myth.

Finding Nemo is a classic movie that demonstrates the light or positive side of fathering. In this epic animated movie, we have

---

[1]Andrew Lang, *The Blue Fairy Book* (London: Longmans, Green, and Co., ca. 1889), p. 64.

the character of the clown fish Nemo who gets lost at sea. So who swims across an ocean and has to overcome many obstacles, including sharks, to rescue Nemo? It is his beloved father, Marlin, who does! It is a fairly rare example in the fairy-tale form of a heroic, benevolent father who will do anything to protect and rescue his offspring who find themselves in danger. Wouldn't we all love to have a father like Marlin?

In Chapter 5, we will explore the ideal-father archetype as a prelude to healing our relationship with male energy in Part II of the book. But first, let's take a look at the father-son dynamic.

Chapter Four

※ ※ ※ ※ ※

WOUNDED MEN:
Fatherhood and the
"Hurt Little Boy" Within

Although the primary focus of this book is dealing with the impact of the father wound on women, it is important to also acknowledge the impact on men. *You* may be impacted, too, if you are in a relationship with a man who has father wounds. It may also help you to understand your own father, who likely has unhealed father wounds of his own.

Men suffer in the same way that women do. In fact, the father can be just as significant an influencer for young men and boys and in some ways more so. If you are a woman, perhaps this awareness can help you have more compassion toward the wounded men in your life, whether they are your boss, co-worker, brother, son, uncle, father, or partner.

The truth is we all harbor the same secret wounds and hurts. The difference can be the way in which these wounds present themselves. We say *secret*, because talking about father wounds doesn't happen very openly. It happens in a therapist's room. It is talked about within men's groups, between good friends, and in healing circles. The society we live in doesn't always support openly expressing your vulnerability or "woundedness."

This is a complex issue that requires self-honesty, along with willingness and motivation to change, since children and adults are sometimes left with the long-term effects of a father who is unable to express or manage his emotions, or deal with power and control issues. We will help you through this process.

HISTORICAL PERSPECTIVES ON FATHERHOOD

Fatherhood and the role of fathers have changed through the ages. Understanding the way in which the role of the father has evolved, especially in fairly recent times, can help you understand your own father and *his* father.

In prior eras, the role of fathers was to earn money. When the father would come home from work, his wife dutifully served him dinner and ensured that the children would be quiet and not interrupt his rest.

This hasn't always been the case. Historically, the stereotype of men hunting and women gathering food and looking after children was likely generally true. What may be surprising is that in preagricultural hunter-gatherer societies, men were involved with their children in a protective role, insofar as the children needed to be carried and kept safe.

As humanity changed with the development of agriculture, large extended families began to help with child rearing. Whole families worked side by side in cultivating crops, and fathers may have been away farming for only parts of the day. Women died more often in childbirth, so there were more single fathers raising children.

So far, it sounds like fathers were quite involved with child rearing, and children had close relationships with their fathers. The segregation of the parenting role to one sex appears to have happened in the later part of the industrialization period in the

West. Men had to go away to work, and women tended to their children. This is when stereotypical roles for men and women developed. The impact of two world wars also meant that men were away from children and families, and reinforced gender roles.

This all changed in the late 20th and early 21st centuries. More women have entered the workforce, and some women earn more than some men. There appears to be less stereotypical "men's work" in this current age of technology. As our society has shifted to focus more on indoor activities and working from home, so have men come to stay at home more, and the previously female-dominated domestic front has changed.

Along with these changes in society and changing roles for both men and women, men have experienced tensions and confusion about maintaining a masculine identity. Men struggle with reconciling their role as a caregiver to children, while at the same time fulfilling the expected role of breadwinner.

The good news is that men seem to be finding balance within themselves and are adjusting to the changing roles. It also appears they are enjoying the freedom of being more than a "success object" who earns money.

The new phenomenon of stay-at-home dads has emerged. Today, men's parental rights are being recognized, and the important role they play in a child's development is being acknowledged. As you probably have noticed, the current generation of men is much more involved with parenting their children. Stay-at-home dads are more common and also respected now, and men provide emotional nurturing. It's normal for fathers to read their children bedtime stories, hold their children and rock them to sleep, and comfort their children when they're upset.

This is a healthy trend, as men are learning to balance their masculine and feminine energies. The future does appear bright. Loving, attentive fathers are needed to raise healthy, sensitive boys and girls, often referred to as the Crystal and Rainbow generations.

Have you noticed more sensitive and still masculine men around? Have you noticed more men gathering in groups to work through their issues, in the same way that women have in past?

This reflects changed societal expectations about men expressing emotions and showing vulnerability.

If that doesn't sound like your father, we understand. This historical overview is not to pardon a father's absent or abusive behaviors, but to help you understand the confusion within many men about their roles and what is expected of them.

MALE IDENTITY FORMATION

Men who grow up with absent or abusive fathers can struggle with feeling like a man, or being comfortable with their masculine identity. This is similar to having low self-worth and self-esteem, where men and boys feel like they are not good enough and have little or no value.

Some of the statistics on this issue for men are alarming. Boys who grow up without a father are more likely to:

- Commit suicide

- Run away from home

- Have behavioral issues

- Be involved in rape, drop out of school, or end up in prison

These statistics speak to how fatherless young men may not learn how to respond to authority or regulate their own emotions. They don't have a positive male role model who can teach them boundaries and societal rules.

Andrew: I managed a program that counseled young men and boys who were suspended from school or involved with juvenile justice. There was often an absent father or an ineffective father who wasn't able to provide adequate support, guidance, or boundaries.

I also observed that as boys mature, they need the guidance of a positive father figure to assist in developing a healthy male self-identity and to learn how to be respectful to women.

My clinical social work highlighted the importance of early intervention, and the need for single-parent families to have positive role models and influences for children of both genders. In some cases, "adopting" a trustworthy male into the family can be helpful, through a formal program like Big Brothers Big Sisters, or by encouraging an emotionally healthy male relative or trustworthy male friend to spend time with the mother and children.

From male adults, boys learn how to treat women, form loving relationships, and behave appropriately. Boys form their masculine identity through the connection with other men and boys. Without those healthy connections, boys don't have a good sense of who they are as men or how to act toward women.

MISPLACED BLAME

If you can understand your father's wound or absence from your life, then you may be more compassionate toward him and yourself. You are able to hold yourself and your inner child blameless, as you understand that *you* did nothing wrong. It was simply the impact of your father's wound that was transferred to you.

As children, we may take on the responsibility for how our fathers feel. Our compassionate side wants to help, heal, and love others. In addition to that, as children we feel responsible for things that simply aren't our fault.

Children mistakenly believe they somehow caused their father to be angry or absent. That somehow it was their own fault that their parents separated, or that Dad is emotionally distant or angry. Carrying this sort of belief can lead to co-dependent behavior as an adult, where you feel responsible for your partner's feelings. In truth, the other person is responsible for their own anger. Your father may have left, emotionally disappeared, or divorced because he had issues or concerns that could not be resolved within the family structure.

Understanding and separating your wound from your father's is important. If you don't learn to distinguish what is *his* issue to resolve and what is *yours*, you may become embroiled in unhealthy relationship patterns such as enmeshment (being overly involved with each other).

It appears that the toxicity of the father wound is imparted to the son or daughter almost automatically. Through the unconscious actions of the father, the son or daughter is left with the same wound or gaping emptiness in his or her heart that they could spend a lifetime trying to mend or fill.

Self-help and healing pioneer Louise Hay's recommendation to see your parents as tiny little children who need love can be so helpful. If you have a photograph of your father as a child or an adolescent, this can be a visual aid. Or, try to envision him as a small boy between five and eight years old. This is likely the age when your father learned how to be a "little man"—that is, to love in a conditional way such as "If you behave in a way I approve of, I will love you." At that age, the boy learned that it was unacceptable to cry or to express his emotions. This could also be a time when his own father either left or in some way invalidated him.

As a consequence, he may have imparted that to you and been unable to express his love or vulnerability to you. He may have been mistreated at this age, or he may have had a lonely childhood in which he himself didn't have the loving male role models that he needed in order to develop a balanced masculine energy.

Doreen: I find it helpful to consider my father's challenging upbringing, as my way of understanding and relating to him. While I used to take his standoffish personality personally, I now realize that it's his defense and coping strategy. This helps me to have compassion for him, instead of futilely wishing he'd change into a warm and cuddly man.

Identifying the source of your father's emotional pain can help you to avoid replicating this dysfunctional pattern in your own relationships. Instead of the patterns being unconsciously repeated, you will clearly see them and their connection to your father. This is not to *blame* him, but to *understand* him for the purposes of healing yourself.

DEALING WITH WOUNDED MEN

Understanding, and being more compassionate toward, your father's painful patterns can help you relate to other men in your life. They can be your romantic partners, your work colleagues, or your brothers or brothers-in-law. In truth, many men (including myself, Andrew), have a hurt little boy and a defensive adolescent within them who is, at times, running the show or in control. The adult male you are talking to can instantly regress into that wounded, insecure, and angry child.

It can be challenging if the male in your life hasn't taken the time to examine how these old ways of behaving aren't effective. Most men will feel as though their pride has been hurt if you raise the fact that they are behaving like a child, even if in fact they are!

That's why it's best to talk to the male when he's feeling calmer and more reasonable. You can gently ask him about his childhood and his relationship with his father. Sometimes, though, it may be best to leave this in the hands of a counselor or therapist.

It can be trap for a lot of us to want to fix or heal the men in our lives. While there is a loving intention behind wanting the male to heal, mature, and grow, it can be a form of control. It can also mean that you no longer have the same relationship dynamic. You may find yourself relating to him as a counselor/helper/mentor does to a client/child/dependent.

Although you may not consciously realize it, this motive could be the reason why you may be drawn to someone initially. The healer within you wants to win over the wounded male in your life through being a great listener and offering understanding. These are key skills to have in any relationship. The trap can be if that male looks to you as his source of healing instead of embarking upon his own journey of self-help and self-exploration.

When Wounded Men Lash Out

Some men unconsciously see women as substitute mothers, especially if they had less-than-healthy relationships with their own mothers. Men with "mother wounds" often project their anger; neediness; and fear of being controlled, criticized, or abandoned onto the women in their lives. Understanding this about your boyfriend or husband can help you set boundaries so that the two of you don't morph into having a mother-son relationship.

Often angry words and gestures are actually the way men express their hurt. It is still socially taboo for men to cry, and openly expressing their fears, hurts, and vulnerabilities may lead them to feel ashamed or be shamed by others. Boys are still being told be strong, loud, and tough. It is still culturally ingrained.

A complex interaction of factors, biological as well as social, makes men abusive. This is *not* to excuse abuse in any form, only to see the reasons behind it. Men are conditioned to behave in aggressive ways by seeing how their own fathers behaved. They see their sports heroes, politicians, and business colleagues' attitudes toward women and children and may take on some of their behaviors.

Again, abuse is never justified, and should never be tolerated. If you find yourself in an abusive relationship, please seek help from domestic violence services or other counseling services that can help you to form a safety plan and an exit strategy. If the danger is immediate, then call the police.

Men's Groups

Often men find themselves in therapy because their partners say they will leave them, or they are court-ordered to commence counseling. Although this is not an ideal way to enter counseling, some men benefit from programs designed for those who struggle with anger, abusive behavior, and addiction.

Men are not socially conditioned to perceive counseling as an option. They often cope through drinking alcohol rather than honestly exploring their emotions and looking at what is driving the behavior.

Awareness of male issues, fatherhood issues, and healing the wounded male are becoming mainstream. Although in some movies men's groups are mocked or satirized, a properly run group for men can be a safe environment for healing.

Andrew: I joined a men's group briefly. In those couple of meetings, I found acceptance of my homosexuality among the heterosexual men present. In fact, I found that the issues between heterosexual and homosexual men are often similar.

Nearly all men have doubts and insecurities about themselves. They struggle to define the meaning of masculinity. They may also be confused about what's expected from them in a society where gender roles are changing. Groups such as these can be therapeutic, and simply forming supportive friendships with other men can be healing.

Anger often comes from hurt. Confronting their hurt feelings can make men feel vulnerable. Acknowledging vulnerability is uncomfortable for most people. Admitting vulnerability and hurt and finding ways to address those feelings can aid men in learning new behaviors and new ways to manage anger.

※ ※ ※

The purpose of this chapter was to demonstrate that men are often hurt little boys who need love and compassion. They also need to take responsibility for their anger and learn how to manage it constructively with strategies for dealing with their own hurt. The next chapter examines what a loving and compassionate father looks like, for those of us who didn't have one.

※ ※ ※ ※ ※

Chapter Five

HEALTHY FATHER
FIGURES AND
BALANCED MALE
ENERGY

It's easy to see the ways in which our fathers may have been lacking, either through abuse or neglect, addiction or absence. However, what is it that we were looking for from our fathers that we know we missed out on? Even if we lacked that "ideal father" in childhood, we can actively change our relationship with male energy so that it is balanced and supportive of our desired future.

Healing Attributes of Healthy Fathering: What Were We Looking for from Our Fathers?

In the book *The Blessing: Giving the Gift of Unconditional Love and Acceptance*, John Trent and Gary Smalley list the following five elements of parental care that instill self-worth and emotional well-being:

Meaningful Touch

We all have an innate need for safe and appropriate physical affection. We are programmed as mammals to seek that warmth and contact from both a mother and a father.

The type of touch you receive from a father can be a positive example of what trustworthy, appropriate physical affection from male energy is like. A lot of gay men have reported that they and their fathers didn't have close relationships. Homosexual sons and heterosexual daughters may seek affection from male partners that they did not receive from their fathers.

Similarly, those who aren't hugged or shown physical affection by their dads may become promiscuous or be in an endless series of relationships in their quest to feel loved. They may be attracted to men who are similar to their fathers in an unconscious attempt to win their fathers' love.

A Spoken Message

Children want to hear, consistently, that they are loved. Yet many *don't* hear "I love you" from their fathers.

Andrew: I don't recall those words passing the lips of my father or stepfather growing up. I believe that they did love me in their own ways. It wasn't until recently, though, that I heard my birth father say the words. As discussed previously, men of his generation, born in the '40s and '50s, were not raised to express love verbally. Children were expected to understand and sense they were loved through a man's actions, such as being a provider.

Having a loving parent regularly say that they love you programs that message deep within your subconscious mind. You grow up with an innate sense of your worth and value. You feel appreciated and don't question whether you are lovable or not.

This consistent message of your lovability can set you up for a life of contentment and emotional security. You may be more resilient in the face of rejection from peers and potential partners because you know you're still loved in spite of rejection.

If you were often told you were loved, you can more readily express love to others. This can also help you develop successful relationships and you aren't left with a sense of insecurity. You can also relate to the experience of God's fatherly love, because you know what that feels like.

Of course, there are lot of other factors; however, having a father who is verbally and physically demonstrative of his love in a safe and appropriate way can foster feeling loved for a lifetime.

Attaching High Value

How many of us grew up with a sense that we really mattered?

Andrew: I have experienced low self-esteem for most of my life. I do attribute some of that to a deep underlying sense that I didn't matter somehow. I grew up with a belief that when my mother remarried, somehow my sister and I were "extra baggage" from her first marriage.

Did your father make it a priority to see you, spend time with you, and tell you that you were important to him? There may have been conflicting demands in his life, such as work obligations. It might have been a struggle for your father to find balance with family. Sometimes a sense of his own guilt and shame and low self-worth may have kept your father away from your life entirely.

Or he may not have known how to have civil contact with your mother, after their relationship ended.

As a child, you don't understand that your father is probably hurt and wounded himself and isn't able to verbally express that you matter and that you're a priority. All you see as a child is that your father is busy or in a bad mood or he may be avoiding interacting with the family through his hobbies or by retreating into his "man cave."

Your father in all likelihood didn't do this deliberately to hurt you. He was probably coping with his own emotions in the best way he knew how, which meant sometimes withdrawing. He may have expected you to know that you are worthy because he worked so hard to provide for his family.

Doreen: I experienced this with my own father, who was an only child raised by his mother and aunts. He told me that he concluded that women were the nurturers and men just needed to stay in the background and work. Since my father didn't have much interaction with his own father, he didn't have a role model to know how to nurture me or my brother, nor did he think that doing so was necessary.

Picturing a Special Future

Having a father who believes that you are a child of God or that you are born for a specific or special purpose can help *you* believe in and fulfill your destiny. A father figure can help you identify your gifts and foster or nurture them by giving you positive reinforcement and encouragement to pursue your passions, hobbies, and interests, and endowing your life with a sense of purpose and meaning.

How many of us were left wondering what our life purpose was? I (Andrew) can remember in my teenage years questioning my life and why I was here. I didn't have a positive male figure guiding me or saying things like:

- "Your life matters."

- "You have an innate value."

- "There is a specific blueprint to your life that you only you can fulfill."

- "You have a unique set of gifts, talents, and abilities to share with the world."

- "I am here to help you to explore what your gifts, talents, and abilities are."

How many people heard their father say, "I will support you and encourage you no matter what path you choose"? Usually, children are taught that support is conditional.

Encouragement to excel and to express our full potential is something many of us didn't receive. Often we were encouraged to pursue only what our parents expected of us. Sometimes we end up fulfilling our parents' expectations rather than our own.

Perhaps you came from a family where you were expected to excel academically, and there was pressure to be a lawyer, a doctor, or in some other high-paying profession, which was considered "success" by parental standards.

If you were given the freedom and the encouragement to be who you wanted to be in accordance with your innate gifts, talents, passions, or interests, who would you be? Sometimes we need to try different courses or venture down different career paths, only to find out that they may not be what we thought they were.

In an ideal world, we would be encouraged to simply be and express who we innately are, with the knowledge that we would still be supported regardless. We would be given the opportunity to make mistakes and be told it was okay.

An Active Commitment

Imagine what your life would be like if you'd had a father who was able to provide all that was explained above for you *on a consistent basis*. You would have a solid platform for a successful life and stable emotions and relationships. Of course, this is in an ideal world, and many of us have experienced this only to varying degrees.

Having that consistency and continuity with a loving father figure would help to counteract some of the pain and rejection that we might experience in life. We would have someone to be our champion and who would help us to fulfill our life purpose with continual encouragement and support.

We want to be clear that we are not blaming fathers for their children drifting through life. We are just explaining why this often happens. Blaming doesn't help anything, but understanding the reasons why people feel rudderless can be helpful and therapeutic.

╳ ╳ ╳

In a sense, these are ideal characteristics for a father figure to convey, and there are very few men who are able to exhibit these qualities consistently. Most of us have received a little of this, and others have received *very* little.

We want to remind you that you're not alone on this journey. Many people like you are going through similar circumstances and are feeling the impact of not having a loving father or father figure in their lives. Many are healing or are already healed. People like you have gone on to experience fulfilling relationships, feel a sense of self-worth, and live an empowered life in spite of having had a father who did not meet their needs as a child or adolescent.

In Part II of this book, we will discuss how you can "reparent" yourself, reimagine your childhood, and recover some of these lost facets of paternal care.

FINDING THE IDEAL FATHER OR BALANCED FATHER

So what is it we are all seeking, or yearning for?

Let's break down what an idealized father or balanced father archetype, or simply *father energy*, looks like.

The Healed Father Archetype or Balanced Father

Many of us have an idealized sense of what our fathers should be like. Perhaps we co-opted this ideal from fairy-tale books or television shows. Usually, reality is quite different. If you are reading this book, then it is likely that your father did not meet your needs or expectations.

For many people, the late, great author Wayne Dyer embodied the healed father archetype very well. He had a blend of characteristics that connected him with many people who were seeking a spiritual father in their lives. He was kind and compassionate. He had a warm and friendly masculine energy, also. He demonstrated wisdom and guided millions of people in a clear way. He was very open about his issues with his childhood abuse experiences and his marital concerns. He was on a deep path of healing and spirituality as well.

He was someone who appeared to be firm yet loving in the way he "parented" the souls of so many. It is likely that this was a reason why people related to him. Of course, he was many other things besides a father figure—an excellent teacher and writer, and someone who popularized spiritual truths and principles to inspire others.

But isn't that what we all secretly hope for in a father? Someone who is:

- Inspiring

- Warm

- Approving and encouraging

- A leader (either of a family or work group)

- Protective

- Uplifting and full of wise counsel

- Human (has faults, but consciously working on healing)

In an ideal world, perhaps we would all have a father like Wayne, who would be firm yet loving, wise, and compassionate, and who would model what a healthy version of masculinity is.

Whatever our gender identity, having someone who is like this in our lives would help us to develop a healthy sense of who we are and our self-worth. It is also possible that we would attract more healthy relationships as a result.

BALANCING MASCULINE AND FEMININE ENERGY

Within the father archetype is the *masculine principle* or *masculine energy*. A lot of us with father wounds struggle with balancing our masculine and feminine selves.

Men and women both have these energies. We may take on a more masculine role in life as a way of compensating for the father wound. Alternatively, a strong feminine side without a complementary masculine side can leave us without the ability to take action steps to be effective in the world.

Masculine energy is also found all throughout nature, and it's a necessity for bringing forth new life. If you're a man, it's essential to make peace with your own masculine energy. Cutting yourself off from your masculinity means rejecting yourself. Even the most effeminate man has masculine energy, as do all females.

Doreen: Divine Feminine energy is much needed in this world, to bring about compassion and nurturing. Yet masculine energy is needed too. In fact, to perform any action requires a form of masculine energy. Connected to performing an action is willpower or drive, which are aspects of male energy.

As I wrote about in my book *Divine Magic*, it's necessary to have a balance of both feminine and masculine energies:

- *Feminine energies* help us with creative ideas, epiphanies, intuition, and insights.

- *Masculine energies* give us the courage, strength, and motivation to take our ideas into the world.

It's as if the feminine energy is the artist, and the masculine energy is the manager. Both are equally needed to enable the artist to have a viable creative career. If you ignore one side of your energy equation, you have less access to your own resources.

Father wounds can make you reject your own masculine energy, and thereby lower your motivation and confidence. Healing your father wounds helps you embrace both your inner feminine and masculine sides.

It's the same with Divine Feminine and Divine Masculine spiritual energy. Sometimes those with father wounds only want to connect with the Divine Feminine, so there's a focus upon the goddesses. Yet wouldn't it be nice to also have spiritual support from the Divine Masculine energies of Jesus, Archangel Michael, and Saint Francis? Perhaps while you're healing your father wounds, you can think of them as trustworthy elder brothers who are protecting and helping you.

The way that masculine energy may have shown itself in your life could be the abuse of power, anger, and aggressive behavior. You may have experienced male energy as abusive, cruel, and critical. The masculine energy was expressed as a power imbalance. Or in the case of an absent father, it was completely deficient.

All of these are negative or shadow aspects of male energy, which may have been attributes that your father or father figures expressed.

In contrast, some of the light sides of masculine energy are being a strong leader—being active, resilient, and driven to succeed. The light side of masculine energy is the power and drive within you to achieve everything that you are meant to achieve in this life.

Without this strong sense of healthy masculine energy, whether you are male or female, you could find yourself feeling lackluster, unenthusiastic, or apathetic. Without that healthy relationship with your male energy, you lack the energy and motivation to make empowering choices.

Alternatively, you may have armed yourself against the abuse or fought against the wound, and you may have taken on some negative masculine traits yourself. You could feel uncontrolled anger or find yourself repeating the same abuse or abandonment that you were subjected to growing up.

At this time it may be worth taking an inventory of where you are with regard to the masculine "father" energy within you.

- Are you currently in the slump of having deficient "yang" or male energy?

- Are you prone to angry outbursts that seem to come from out of nowhere (wounded-male energy)?

- Have you internalized the wounded-male aspect of yourself, turning anger toward yourself that you may experience as depression or as feeling unworthy, powerless, and victimized?

Developing healthy male energy by healing the father wound can help you feel empowered, balanced, and whole. You will feel a healthy drive and ambition to be able to create and follow through on your goals and ambitions.

Father energy and male energy are obviously connected. As you uncover the father wound within you and honestly look at the way your male energy may be out of balance, this can set you on the path of healing and balancing yourself.

Healthy father energy and male energy can result in you manifesting new opportunities, and the world will appear to be more abundant and giving. The action of giving is a male quality or attribute. The healthy father energy is generous and gives freely from the heart. Having a healthy relationship with your own male energy will allow you to feel empowered to take action to increase your own levels of prosperity, and consequently be able to give to others, including yourself.

This is fundamental for a successful life on this earth. The male energy is needed to propel you forward and to keep you looking ahead rather than feeling like you are either stuck or looking back over past events that have hurt you.

Healing your relationship with the Divine Masculine and with men in general will mean that you are at peace with 50 percent of the population, and you can be free to live the life that you want unencumbered and free.

❈ ❈ ❈

Part I of this book was designed to bring conscious awareness of the patterns that come with the father wound. We hope that instead of repeating the same old unhealthy ways of dealing with pain, you will open doors to healing pathways that are appropriate for you—a topic we will turn to next in Part II.

❈ ❈ ❈ ❈ ❈

PART II

HEALING THE PAIN

Chapter Six

Bringing Your Emotions into the Light

We've written at length about how the father wound has impacted your life, self-esteem, and relationships . . . so what can you *do* about it? The good news is that there are a range of techniques and healing methods that you can use to move on with your life.

So how do you know which technique or approach is right for you? Well, you might feel drawn to a particular page. You could feel an inner *yes* or knowing, or your eyes might naturally feel drawn to a section title. Your heart or gut may also feel a "tug" toward trying out some technique.

Please view Part II and its explanations as a guide and listen to your own intuition to work out what particular technique or blend of techniques is appropriate for you. In a sense, this is like a banquet or buffet of ideas, strategies, and ways to move forward on your healing journey.

These chapters are not intended to be a replacement for therapy or counseling. The techniques in them can be used in conjunction with a therapist. If you are feeling distressed while working through any chapter, please be kind to yourself and take a break, and come back to it when you are feeling centered. And if you feel the need for spiritual support, Part III offers ways to connect with Divine energy for comfort and healing.

If you have thoughts of self-harm, then please immediately call a crisis hotline and seek lifesaving professional help. Remember: *You are needed upon this earth—otherwise you wouldn't be here.* You can also help others to heal from the type of pain and grief that you've experienced, or become involved in child abuse–prevention campaigns. In this way, all of your suffering becomes the basis of blessings for the world.

BREAKING FEAR-BASED PATTERNS

The sooner we can all take the brave step of noticing our inner-child patterns, the sooner we can move into healing and wholeness. This comes from acknowledging our woundedness and taking steps such as those suggested in these chapters.

At times, you may have attempted to escape your pain through co-dependent relationships, addictions, and choosing partners who are significantly older than you are. You aren't alone in making these choices. They are an indicator that perhaps you have a father wound that is unacknowledged.

Father wounds remain active within your psyche whether you acknowledge them or not. You can see evidence of your father wound by noticing the "triggers" that send you emotionally back to your childhood.

Acknowledging and working through your unpleasant feelings is vital to breaking fear-based patterns. In fact, these emotions carry with them a healing elixir. As you feel, express, and release the grief and anger and shed tears of sadness, jealousy, and rage, you make room for the healing balm of acceptance, forgiveness, peace, and love to enter and take up residence in the space your father wound previously occupied. Many of us are walking around with grief bottled up and stuffed down within us and our energy field. We don't have to live this way when therapeutic and spiritual help is readily available.

Reactions to Authority Figures

A lot of healing comes from self-awareness and being honest with yourself about your feelings and reactions. For example, notice how you emotionally react to male authority figures such as politicians, corporate leaders, police officers, and so forth.

If your blood pressure and heart rate increase just from thinking of male authority figures, your stress responses are activated by perceived dangers.

Imagine that you're lying down on a sofa and talking with your nonjudgmental best friend about your reactions to thinking of male authority figures. Ask yourself:

- *How old was I when I first reacted to male authority figures this way?*
- *What was happening at that time?*
- *Who was with me?*
- *How did I react?*
- *How did the other people with me react?*

Doreen: For example, I was triggered by grouchy men because my own father expresses anger nonverbally rather than directly. He is the silent type who avoids feeling or discussing emotions, so you can't have productive conversations to clear anger.

I didn't realize how much this process had hurt me until I noticed my pattern of reacting to moody or grumpy men. I would immediately revert into my frightened little-girl self, feeling powerless and out of control. I'd sometimes become passive-aggressive, making sideways comments about their grouchiness instead of directly having conversations about it. I'd leave relationships with grouchy men, instead of healing or understanding them.

Once I saw the pattern, my little girl immediately handed the torch of responsibility to my adult self. I can now talk directly and assertively to a man whom I perceive as angry, without the quivering-in-my-boots fears. Awareness really is our friend!

Roller-Coaster Relationships

Some people would rather be in dysfunctional or unhappy relationships than be single. Other people bounce from one relationship to the next without taking stock of why the first failed.

Having some space and time alone is important to process what happened in the previous relationship. It may seem difficult to take the time to face your feelings, such as fear of aloneness or abandonment, before seeking out a new relationship.

By doing so, you can drop all the old baggage, heal those broken wings, and fly toward a future of hope and loving relationships, free from the past. This is a happier alternative to leaving one partner who unconsciously reminds you of your father, and then entering into the next relationship with the same issues. Facing the underlying wounds can help you to break the cycle of relationships that crash and burn when you realize you're with someone who's like your father.

As we discussed previously, trauma survivors are often addicted to drama and the highs of adrenaline from being in a roller-coaster relationship. Plus, if all you've ever known growing up is drama, you may feel uncomfortable in a calm and stable relationship.

Healing this pattern means having the willingness to date nice men whom you're not necessarily attracted to at first. It means getting accustomed to being with a guy who buys you presents, who respects you, and who keeps his promises. You deserve this great guy and a healthy monogamous relationship!

Prayer can help you to recalibrate the type of men you're attracted to and whom you attract. Pray sincerely for help in becoming attracted to nice men and enjoying a quieter form of excitement.

Doreen: I did this after suffering in relationships with men who were abusing alcohol and drugs. Although I was sober, I was co-dependently enabling my partners by sharing in their justifications for getting high and drunk. I would excuse their behavior and suffer through being with someone who was intoxicated.

My entire focus was upon "making" my partner happy, until one day I realized how controlling that intention is. I also saw that a person has to choose to be happy themselves. And my biggest Aha! moment was seeing that I was still trying to win my father's approval and please him through my "substitute dad," my romantic partner.

I finally connected this to my father wound of having a dad who was emotionally absent. While he has been sober as long as I can remember, his addiction to workaholism is his defense for pushing people away. I remember going into his office as a child, and our conversations were invariably centered around his work.

So I chose romantic partners who also pushed away emotional connections with a different form of addiction. Instead of workaholics, they were abusers of alcohol and drugs. My normal recourse was to try couples therapy, and when that didn't work, I'd leave.

Finally, I grew tired of this unhealthy pattern and put my foot down to the universe. I prayed fervently to never again be attracted to an addict . . . and it worked! I'm now in a long-term, committed, happy, sober relationship with a man who is in touch with his emotions, who readily admits when he goes into his ego, and who loves having discussions about his feelings. (And yes, he is heterosexual!)

When our hurt inner child takes over our adult consciousness, it is calling out for healing and acknowledgment. Once you consciously see the *connections between your father wound and same way that your boss, partner, brother, or other man is mistreating you,* then you can make a choice to address it with the healing methods described herein.

BRAVELY FACING YOUR FEELINGS

Life events involving the father wound keep recurring so that you will pay attention to what is going on and take some time to heal. If we stay busy and pretend that everything is okay, the wounds never get identified or healed.

Fear of Being Alone

Andrew: As I sit here writing this book, I have had to face uncomfortable feelings alone. Solitude has triggered many issues that have resurfaced. Yet confronting them is a necessary part of my therapeutic process, as it is for yours.

Being comfortable in your own skin and with being alone is a key strength you can develop over time. Sure, we are social beings and we need human interaction, but we believe in having a balance.

Finding solace by going out in nature, writing about your feelings in a journal, praying, or expressing yourself through drawing and painting are all self-care activities that you can do on your own.

Doreen: If you are going to be alone on a Friday or Saturday night (a time when many people go out on the town), do something nice for yourself. Planning ahead can prevent you from sulking or wallowing in your feelings. Decide to cook a lovely meal for yourself, watch a funny or entertaining movie, or create a spa-like sea-salt and essential-oil bath with candles. Enjoy a good book or magazine. Or, take yourself out for a date! Go enjoy a meal or an event.

I remember a time when it was frowned upon for women to go to restaurants by themselves. Thank goodness that stigma is gone! Lots of men and women now comfortably dine solo.

I once went to see the musician Sting when I was traveling by myself to give a workshop in a city where he was having a concert. I had a lovely time, and easily connected with the concertgoers sitting in my row.

Other people cope with *loneliness*, which is different from being alone, by seeking contact through online chat. Although Facebook and other sites can be great for staying in touch, they're not a substitute for real-life friendships and connections.

So how do you face your fears or deal with feeling lonely? Honestly acknowledging your lonely feelings is the starting point. Admit them to yourself, and know that being alone or lonely is not a condemnation of who you are. There are many fine people who would love to be your friend. It's just a matter of knowing that you deserve healthy and loving friendships. We will help you to get there!

Also, look at what else is going on in your thinking. Sometimes it is a belief that you are unlovable or unworthy. Is it possible that you have pushed people away because of fears that they would reject you? We've all done this. There's no shame. This is about taking a self-inventory to see what patterns you want to keep, and what you don't want to keep.

Andrew: I have felt lonely for most of my life. Writing this book has made me face my fears and those unpleasant feelings. Yes, it's tempting to eat something unhealthy or do something else that isn't good for you instead of facing your feelings; however, that only serves to mask instead of heal your emotions.

Facing your darkest fears, such as believing that you will be alone for the rest of your life or that no one likes or loves you, can be uncomfortable. But they loosen their grip on you as you shine the light of awareness upon them.

Avoidance

Andrew: This book took a very long time to write because I didn't want to face my feelings a lot of the time. At first I believed that this meant I was just procrastinating, a word I dislike because it basically means avoidance. I went weeks without writing much or researching the topic. It was a form of writer's block, and I had to work out what the block was about.

I didn't want to look at my past or acknowledge pain and uncomfortable feelings that were sitting beneath the surface. I used to say things to myself like, *My childhood wasn't that bad.* It's true; many people probably have had worse childhoods. Yet it's important not to diminish your pain or compare your wound to other people's.

Everyone is unique and has their own sensitivity levels. We are all affected by father wounds in different ways.

Examining the painful consequences of your father wound is no fun. If you find yourself wanting to grab a snack, tackle some housework, or do something else to distract yourself, you are not alone. I also found myself using all sorts of diversions to avoid facing the pain of my past.

In a way, a part of your mind is attempting to protect itself. Avoidance is a behavior that is trying to keep you safe. Yet it's not safe to avoid necessary healing work.

Feeling Like You're Stuck in the Past

Another reason why writing this book took longer than expected was the thought *This is all in the past.* You may tell yourself (or someone else may say), "Why don't you just move on?"

If you are new to the journey of self-healing or if you've told friends and family that you're embarking on a journey of healing the father wound, you're likely to have some people tell you, "That's all in the past; just let it go."

Historically that is what most people did before therapy became popular. If it were so easy to move on, you would have done that already. Unfortunately, what "moving on" means for most people is basically blocking old memories or repressing them.

A lot of people are good at putting on a brave face or wearing a "mask" of happiness or being okay, when underneath they feel inadequate and they've buried their feelings.

We know now that suppression of emotions is unhealthy. Overly focusing on them is unhealthy too. However, there is a difference between bravely spending some time examining your feelings with the intent of releasing them and wallowing in your past with "pity parties."

Facing your feelings also means you will have to answer a couple of tough questions that come up during father therapy:

"SHOULD I SEE MY FATHER OR NOT?"

The question arises about how to deal with your father. Should you avoid him or see him? As you're going through the emotional healing process, it may be helpful to distance yourself from him until you feel stronger.

A woman named Lucy felt enraged that her father who'd abused her now needed her care in his elderly declining health. She'd previously confronted her father about the abuse, and he'd downplayed and dismissed it. So Lucy felt angry each time she was with her father, especially when he implied that she "owed" him the care. The sense of entitlement put Lucy over the edge, and she finally consulted a therapist trained in trauma recovery. The therapist gave Lucy support as she transitioned her father's care to a nurse practitioner. Now Lucy doesn't feel used by her father, and her therapist has helped her to release her anger and guilt in healthy ways.

If family get-togethers, such as the holiday season, weddings, or graduations, are emotional triggers for you, here are some helpful ways to care for yourself:

Know that you don't need to attend every family function, especially if your relatives' behavior is verbally abusive or harsh, or if it threatens your sobriety. You can choose to spend the holidays with healthy friends who love and support you. You may need therapeutic support to deal with any guilt or grief that you feel in missing family get-togethers.

Plan your family visits to be short and sweet. You don't need to stay for hours, especially if some family members become intoxicated as the evening wears on. Making an appearance at a family function is often enough to satisfy everyone's need to see each other.

Help the family get-together to be less stressful. For example, hold the function at your house to ensure no alcohol is served. Play calming meditative music. Seat feuding relatives at different tables, or invite them separately to different functions.

If the gathering triggers you emotionally, then go for a walk, or go into the bathroom to sit down and pray for help.

Carry a talisman with you to help you keep your adult identity, such as a symbol of a work project that reminds you that you're an adult now.

If you live with your father, or there's an occasion to see him one-on-one, you have choices about how to handle the situation:

- **Avoidance.** Some people choose to "divorce" their abusive parent, because the parent isn't capable of speaking or acting respectfully.

- **Meeting with a family therapist.** A professional neutral party can help clarify communication and avoid abusive behavior.

- **Catharsis.** Write out your feelings in a letter to your father (that you won't send to him) as a way of reducing the fury and rage so that you can have a civil conversation with him.

- **Confrontation.** This involves telling your father exactly how you feel. Most of the time, this method results in the father denying or defending his actions unless he has spent time in therapy and is now more aware. If you can share your feelings in a softer, more assertive way (instead of steamrolling him with your years of anger), he's more likely to hear you.

- **Pretending like all is well**. This method is unhealthy for both people. Stuffing down feelings can result in illness and addictions, and your father doesn't have the opportunity for helpful feedback that could allow him to grow and learn.

- **Prayer**. Prayer really does work and is helpful in your decision-making about what steps to take with your father.

- **Assertiveness**. This involves you staying strong in your adult self, and speaking your truth to your father until you both clear the issue. This is the ideal; however, please know that this may take some practice on your part if you're not accustomed to having honest conversations with your father. In the case of a father who is dying, this is the best method for having that "final conversation," which can help both of your souls.

"DO I SHARE MY JOURNEY WITH OTHERS?"

As you go on your healing journey, the urge to share about your wounds can be strong. At times, you may want to tell someone you just met or in a work environment how awful your father or childhood was. These aren't the best places to air your hurts and your wounds. Therapeutic groups and counseling practices are more appropriate places to do this. They are environments where people are trained and other participants within the group are also there to support you.

You don't want to burden your friends all the time with your challenges. Some probably won't want to hear about your father issues. It can be a conversation killer, because they are probably facing the same pain and don't want to deal with it. They are likely caught up in the denial stage of their own grief.

Yes, there are likely dear friends who can offer a sympathetic ear for you on occasion. Yet having a counselor or a therapist who can be objective and help with coping strategies can be very heal-ing, and then you aren't burdening your friends.

Andrew: I still talk with friends occasionally about what is going on; however, I do that from a space of having already pro-cessed the issue, which is different from "dumping" or placing the burden on someone else.

If you are able to heal these issues with the help of these groups and hopefully this book, you will be more effective at work, and you will be more present with your friends and within relation-ships. Without awareness of these dynamics, there is a tendency to replay these old family scenarios within relationships at work and to seek validation from peers.

⚜ ⚜ ⚜ ⚜ ⚜

Chapter Seven

WORKING THROUGH
THE GRIEF

As you read this book, you may be experiencing strong feelings. Grief is one of those things that can sneak up on you unexpectedly. This is especially true if you've tried to stifle or avoid feeling sadness, loss, fear, and anger. In fact, it could be your inner child trying to gain your attention through these feelings. Dialoguing with your inner child will be discussed in more detail in a later chapter.

A key to mending your father wound is to allow and express emotions such as sadness, loneliness, disconnection from the world, deprivation, or anger at not having the father you wanted. You may be feeling one of these things or cycle between feeling the sadness, loss, and anger. You may feel cheated, like you missed out on something vital. We understand; in fact, we have felt the pangs of loss and envy when seeing loving fathers interacting with their children. Combined with that, there is a "pang" that is felt in the heart and a yearning to have that need fulfilled.

STAGES OF GRIEF

The well-known five stages of grief as described by Elisabeth Kübler-Ross also relate to grieving the loss of a healthy relationship with your father. These are broad categories designed to help you to understand your process a bit more. Grief can be tricky, and complex emotions can occur simultaneously. Emotional healing is a process rather than a destination. It can be like peeling layers off an onion. Once you work through one emotion, another surfaces.

While this can seem like an endless process, you will experience longer and longer periods of peace and tranquility. The goal of working through the stages of grief is to find a sense of peace with what occurred between you and your father. In a sense, at a certain level, you integrate what occurred with who you are now. That can mean that the wound is still there but doesn't dominate your thoughts and feelings as much as it used to.

Stage 1: Denial and Isolation

Many people live their lives avoiding intimacy and remaining fairly isolated as a result of having a father wound. There can be a fear of replicating the abusive or dysfunctional relationship that you had with your father in a new relationship. Isolation is a way of protecting yourself from further pain; however, it can get lonely and is not good for long periods of time.

Denial occurs when we repeat patterns in relationships and we pretend that nothing's wrong, and any problems are the other person's fault. We deny playing a part in this co-creation. Denial of the father wound can mean that it goes underground and remains active within your unconscious mind. It influences your choices and the vibration you send out to the universe, until you choose to bring it into the light of conscious awareness, as we discussed in the last chapter.

Denying that you have a father wound can be a way of protecting yourself and avoiding difficult emotions or remembering traumas.

Denial, while initially protective, can stop you from dealing with the issue at hand.

Mary went from one troublesome relationship to the next. With each partner, she found herself having communication difficulties and things didn't last. Mary spoke with a counselor, who asked her what her relationship was like with her father. Mary admitted that it was difficult, and she had trouble communicating with him.

Initially, Mary didn't want to examine the link to her challenging adolescence. She denied that her current issues were related to her past. Over time, Mary was able to face the pain of feeling misunderstood by her father. Mary's counselor advised her on the different ways men and women communicate. She came to understand her father better, and later she noticed that her friendships and relationships also improved.

In some ways, denial is the most pernicious stage—and the one most people find themselves at with their father wound. Reading this book means that you've already made a choice to recover this lost part of yourself and return to wholeness. Well done, and congratulations for getting this far and being willing to face your feelings. Willingness is key to healing.

Stage 2: Anger

Anger is a tricky emotion that can be challenging to grasp because it can be socially unacceptable to feel it. Women in particular are taught not to express this emotion. Yet it's normal to feel angry or resentful toward your father for not giving the love you craved as a child.

It's normal for the anger to be turned inward as well. As a child, you may have blamed yourself for not being good enough to warrant your father's affection. You may have had unrealistic expectations to live up to. Intellectually, you know that it's not your fault, yet children often blame themselves anyway. Many of us still have that angry inner child who feels ashamed, abandoned, unlovable, or vengeful because of their unhealed relationship with their father.

Often anger masks other emotions, such as hurt or powerlessness. Many children learn to fit into society by hiding their anger. This is true in dysfunctional families who are more concerned with appearing perfect to others than with facing and healing their issues. So children are taught to behave as if nothing's wrong, and put on a good show of perfection for the neighbors to admire.

Anger can also show itself through passive-aggressive sarcasm or acting-out behavior. Unfortunately, put-down "humor" and speaking harshly are considered to be almost a normal way of communicating. This can seem fun for a while, but in reality, words do wound and sarcasm pushes people away.

Jill was using anger as a shield. At work, colleagues found her unapproachable and quite intimidating. Jill admitted that anger actually made her feel powerful. She later realized that she was using this emotion as a shield to keep herself safe, yet it also made her feel lonely.

Jill was able to let her guard down when she was talking with good friends, who had the courage to tell her that they found her to be edgy and unfriendly. She was able to open up about her childhood experiences with men—including her father—abusively violating her boundaries. Jill was able to see how anger served her as a protective measure.

Initially, a lot of us can swing into anger when we are processing what happened to us as a child. *How could they have done this to me? How could they do this to a child?* are the indignant realizations. This resentment, although justified, can harden into a habit of bringing anger into every conversation as a "Don't hurt me!" message. This keep-away energy does serve as a warning to would-be abusers; however, it also repels gentle people away from you, too.

Stage 3: Bargaining

This is that stage when we may bargain with ourselves and with God as a way of coping with the father wound. An example of this is thinking, *If only I had been a better son or daughter, then my father would not have left me and Mom.*

Another example of bargaining is, *If I am a superwoman and achieve a lot in my career, then God will bring my father back and will heal me and my pain.* The truth is that you are worthy regardless of your father's presence or absence and that God can and does heal you regardless of what you achieve.

Bargaining can be something that we do without being consciously aware we are doing it. Besides overachieving, it could take the form of repetitive prayers such as "If I do this for You, God, will You please return that special lover [father figure] back into my life?"

Yet another way in which bargaining can show up in your life as a result of having father issues could be negotiating with yourself: "If I can just be more loving or if I can be the perfect person, then I will meet the perfect guy."

Marcy was a single mother. Becoming pregnant at a young age had made her life very challenging, and she recalled believing that God was punishing her for her actions. Marcy turned to religion to try to make peace with God and her wild past. She had previously rejected religion, yet she had pressure from her family to return to a conventional spirituality. Marcy spent a lot of time trying to atone for what she was told were sinful actions. She went to confession, prayed, and pleaded with God to please forgive her for her transgressions. She believed that if she said the right prayers and kept good company, God would eventually reward her with a loving, supportive partner and that her life would change.

Marcy eventually realized that bargaining with God doesn't work. She had to learn to become happy with herself and her own life. So she decided to further her education. She took up part-time work as well. Marcy found a supportive church that cast no judgments on her about her past or any of her actions. Marcy eventually made peace with herself, and a friendly-looking man caught her eye one Sunday. Without resorting to bargaining, she was able to create a positive future for herself with a caring partner who didn't replicate her father's patterns and was a wonderful father figure to her child.

Stage 4: Depression

Feeling sad when you realize that you have missed out on having a loving father figure is normal. Sadness is a feeling. Depression is a clinical diagnosis. How can you tell if you are depressed? You feel sad most of the time. Your mood and appetite change. You don't enjoy the things you usually enjoy doing. You may eat excessively or less frequently. Depression affects everyone differently.

You may have trouble with sleep. Usually if you have trouble falling asleep, that can be a form of anxiety. If you wake up early and are unable to get back to sleep, that can be a symptom of depression.

If you are feeling sad, please acknowledge these feelings. If you have supportive friends, do call on them. Your true friends won't judge you for being sad. They may encourage you to join in fun group activities with them. You may not feel like doing anything and may need to push yourself a little to go for a walk or go out for lunch with friends. Sometimes you have to act first and you feel better later.

Andrew: I am not a health practitioner; however, for mild symptoms of depression and anxiety, I have found the following supplements to be helpful: SAM-e, DHA (fish oil or flaxseed oil), 5-HTP, Saint-John's-wort, and magnesium. If you are taking antidepressants, these supplements may interact with them, so please consult with your prescribing physician and seek out a natural health practitioner to help you to choose a combination that is right for you. Essential oils—such as lemon, orange, peppermint, and rose—can also help uplift your mood.

If you feel like crying, cry. Tears can cleanse you and help relieve sadness and tension. If you find yourself sobbing uncontrollably for long periods and you don't feel lighter afterward, then you could be tipping toward depression.

If your symptoms strongly persist for a period of two weeks or more, then it may be time to seek professional help, which is advisable for depression and anxiety, especially in severe forms of these conditions. Please seek it out if you notice your mood is dangerously low and you are thinking of ending your life. Suicide is a permanent way of trying to fix an often-temporary problem. If you are feeling suicidal or have an urge to harm yourself, please immediately call a suicide hotline for support. A good counselor, crisis hotline, or support group can help you through challenges and restore your happiness.

A woman named Rose was feeling very sad after her last breakup. Each time a relationship ended, she was reminded of the way that her father walked out of her life at a young age. She found that she was spending long periods of time alone and eating a lot of chocolate. Rose stopped returning phone calls. She no longer enjoyed going out with her friends, instead using her time alone to journal.

Rose realized that her choice of music impacted her mood, so she opted to listen to more uplifting music. She also reached out for support online. Eventually, she decided that these feelings had gone on for too long and that it was time to take action. Rose found that talking to a therapist and taking some supplements helped her. She pushed herself to exercise. She found that once she started walking, her mood improved, especially when she was outside near water. With the help of her therapist, she identified the beliefs from childhood that contributed to her sadness and was able to work through them.

Stage 5: Acceptance

Acceptance means that you have come to terms with what you have experienced. This doesn't mean that you condone or excuse the abusive or abandoning behavior. It also doesn't mean that your grief or healing has been completed. It means you feel more peaceful and have integrated the experiences within yourself to some extent. Sometimes you can stay in this space for a while; at other times, you may find you cycle through the other stages.

Enjoy those periods of time when you feel as though you have integrated your wound to some degree. That means that you are aware of the scar and the damage done to your self-worth or self-esteem; however, you have accepted that experience into your life. The pain may never go away fully, yet you become more aware of the other parts of yourself as you process your issues with the techniques in this book or any others that you have discovered for yourself.

Accepting yourself and wherever you are is helpful to do regardless of what stage of healing you find yourself in. Acceptance of your wounds, quirks, and idiosyncratic behaviors fully can allow you to move past them. You will notice that some unhelpful emotions or patterns of behavior become less prevalent, the hurt feelings become less intense, and you feel more whole or in control and balanced.

The more you accept yourself and focus on your strengths, talents, and abilities, the more you draw out other aspects of yourself.

Andrew: A lot of factors contributed to my low self-esteem, including growing up in a church that didn't accept my homosexuality. I also felt abandoned and rejected by my father and many people in my life. Searching for love and acceptance, I spent years in the commercial gay-bar culture. I enjoyed the freedom, as well as rebelling against my oppressive past.

After some time of doing this, though, I still felt alone. Friends and lovers didn't stick around. I also found that I didn't fit into the same circle of gay friends anymore. I craved genuine heart-to-heart connections rather than one-night stands. One night I really hit bottom with my painful feelings. I was so tired of feeling bad about myself, and I was also desperate for a way to numb my emotions.

Suddenly, I was startled by the appearance of Jesus in a blue robe sitting on my sofa. I kept looking and the figure still sat there. I heard a voice, which I assumed to be Jesus's, say, "If you continue to do what you are doing, then you are on a downward slide out of which you may not make it."

I knew what Jesus meant: stop running away from myself, and stop trying to numb my feelings. I then heard beautiful angelic voices telling me that I was loved and was a sacred being. The angelic voices continued to speak in a loving, nonjudgmental way, saying that I had a life purpose to fulfill.

The experience was so uplifting and ecstatic that I started laughing with joy. I couldn't believe what was happening, but it was so powerful and real that it could not be passed off as a hallucination.

This became a turning point in my life. I realized that being gay wasn't wrong or bad. After all, Jesus just appeared to me and was praying on my behalf. I learned that God, Jesus, and the angels don't condemn anyone, no matter what! I also learned to align my heart with my actions. That's when I began to explore spiritual communities and churches that didn't judge my sexuality. I accepted that Jesus and the angels were there for me, too. More importantly, I was able to look in the mirror with love and accept every facet of myself and my life.

We believe that God, Jesus, and the angels are available to anyone who reaches out and asks for help. We all have freedom as to how we choose to express this powerful energy. Everyone is different and has an inner knowing about what is right for them.

A word of caution with doing therapy or any form of self-help is that you may feel like you are swamped by negative feelings or that feelings of hurt begin to take over your personality. It is important to realize that you are so much more than your wound and your hurt feelings.

You are a Divine child of God who is *worthy* simply because you exist. This may be difficult to accept. However, as you work through the feelings of shame, guilt, and undeservingness through gentle acceptance, you begin to find out what else is present within your being. You discover the precious gem that you are, and in fact, your father wound can be a doorway or pathway to discovering your strengths and abilities.

❁ ❁ ❁

Once again, it is important to note that these stages are not linear or sequential. Our emotions tend to fluctuate through these stages. They are a rough guide that is meant to inform you about where you may find yourself while working through grief associated with father wounds. Please adapt this to your own situation.

As we mentioned, the stages of grief can occur simultaneously. You will probably experience them in your own unique way. That said, in our experience people with father wounds tend to particularly struggle with processing anger, so in the next chapter we will look at techniques to work through "stuckness" at this critical stage.

While you are in this healing space, please be gentle with yourself. It's okay to put this book aside for a while and come back to it when you are feeling stronger. If we knew any other way to heal, we would have found it.

We believe the following techniques will bring about rapid healing with minimal discomfort to you. If you find the process overwhelming, please stop. You may also want to talk to a therapist or counselor along the way who can help you if you find yourself feeling stuck or having difficulty processing the pain.

Chapter Eight

❁ ❁ ❁ ❁ ❁

WORKING THROUGH ANGER

Acknowledging anger is the first step to getting past it. Allow yourself to feel that emotion and vent it appropriately. As we will discuss in this chapter, venting can involve beating pillows or a mattress, yelling in your car (with windows closed), or writing a scathing letter. (Please don't send this letter.)

The purpose of such an exercise is to let out the emotions that are bottled up within you and your energy system. Your intention is to safely express and release the anger. Once you do so, you create space to replace it with feelings such as peace, acceptance, and forgiveness. You may then want to do the healing work with your inner child discussed in Chapter 10.

Your inner child may feel anger at what happened to you growing up. This is not a "pretty" emotion, and most of us are good at burying the feeling. If you experienced abuse as a child, you didn't know what to feel or how to handle and process your feelings, especially if the abuse occurred when you were very young.

It's natural to feel outraged that you were violated by those whom you trusted! The anger probably also extends to your mother who did not provide you with protection. In addition, like many abuse survivors, you may feel anger toward yourself, especially if the abuser blamed you during the abusive experiences.

Many abuse survivors fear that if they allow their anger to be expressed, they will lose control and break things or say regrettable words. Yet our experience as clinicians shows that feeling your underlying anger is calming, instead of enraging. It's like letting air out of an overfilled balloon. If you are able to get in touch with your anger, then you are on your way toward healing.

Rage can be a messy or "tricky" emotion, and you may want to work with an anger group. Workshops, retreats, and groups for men and women can provide a safe environment with skilled practitioners who can guide you to finding constructive expressions of anger. A therapist or counselor can also assist you in processing this emotion.

Studies on trauma recovery find that it's best to alternate your focus on anger with letting yourself rest and be calm to allow the healing process to happen at its own pace.

CATHARSIS AND RELEASE WORK

Physically expressing your anger and rage by hitting a mattress, pillows, or punching bag with your fists or a bat can help. This is called *catharsis*. Making sounds while you do so is important. Please cathart privately with windows closed so neighbors don't get concerned. If you can go somewhere in nature where no one can hear you, even better. Some people punch the seat and yell in their car with the windows up. Other people go to the seashore to pound the sand and yell near the crashing waves.

Getting this toxic energy out of your body and your energy field is important. Your inner child will feel much happier at having this emotion processed and expressed. It may come to you in waves initially, and it will dissipate because your intention is to express it and release it. Remember to not bottle the anger inside.

Trauma-recovery experts advise that releasing pent-up emotions needs to be done in short increments, with intervals of pleasant distractions. Do some catharsis such as screaming or pounding in a safe way, and then do something enjoyable. The mind isn't ready to dump and heal everything in one day, even if you wish you could unload it all immediately. Healing father wounds is a process, just like other forms of healing.

Angelic Anger Release

Expressing the anger can make you feel initially very energized and help to shift lethargy or depression. Allow this powerful energy to swirl through each of your energy centers and ask for your anger to be released safely, peacefully, and with ease.

"Thank you, guardian angels and Archangel Michael, for clearing the anger that was held within my energy body."

Afterward, you can actually feel empty and tired. Replacing anger with Divine love and light is important. In Matthew 12:43–45, Jesus emphasized that if we only release negativity and don't occupy that space up with God's love, even more negativity will come and fill in the void. So it's essential to pray for God's presence to fill you up after you do releasement work.

"Dear God, thank You for filling me up with Your Divine loving presence, and protecting me from negativity."

Creative Therapies

Clay work, sand-tray therapy, and art therapy can be fun and creative ways to heal anger and rage. Someone trained in creative therapies can assist you by going through a specific sequence to transform the anger.

Or you can work with clay on your own: Simply grab a ball of clay and throw it on the ground or onto a board. You can make a sound as you do so, such as "Arrr!" or "Braa!" and the clay itself makes a satisfying *splat* noise. It might seem strange, but this is a quick and safe way of expressing anger and getting it out of your system. Just be sure to reach out for support if the anger feels overwhelming.

Having thoughts of revenge is normal. Acknowledging dark fantasies that you may have is okay to do, *as long as you don't act upon them.* It's best to pray for a safe and healthy way to release these vengeful thoughts. EMDR counseling can also help to reduce post-trauma flashbacks, which can trigger these fantasies.

Anger can be a mobilizing energy that can move you into action. You can channel anger into activism, for example, or by helping other people who are experiencing what you have been through. Anger can help with dislodging some heavy and depressing feelings. In that way, it can serve as a healing force, as long as you don't take those feelings out on others.

Effective Communication

Doreen: In my book *Assertiveness for Earth Angels,* I describe a "middle ground" way of communicating your needs to others.

For example, we can tell our friend or partner, "I feel frustrated/confused when you speak to me like that. I wonder if we can both take the tone down and speak more respectfully to each other." It can feel unnatural at first. Over time you can learn to regulate your reactions to others.

Initially a protective device, anger can become a habit over time. Learning to do things such as walking away briefly and calming yourself through deep breathing can help. Come back to a discussion when you are feeling more calm. Meditation and cultivating peaceful emotions through listening to relaxing music can help as well. A useful meditation to do is Louise Hay's *Anger Releasing,* or you might want to try my *How to Let Go and Forgive* meditation and teaching video.

HEALING ANGER TOWARD YOUR FATHER

One of the ways to arrive at a measure of peace is through forgiveness. Forgiveness does not mean that what someone did to you as a child, adolescent, or adult is okay. It is, however, a way of releasing yourself from the emotional prison where you can find yourself. Holding on to feelings of resentment and anger can actually make you feel safe initially, but over time, they can imprison you.

Forgiveness is finding the key to your prison. You may feel some apprehension in actually putting the key into the lock. That can be because you don't want your father or the person who hurt you to get away with it. You may still be harboring thoughts of punishment.

Forgiveness does *not* mean condoning, excusing, or forgetting the abusive action. Neither does it mean that you have to hang out with the person and risk getting hurt again. It means that you are no longer willing to carry toxic anger within your body, mind, or emotions. Forgiveness is the ultimate detox.

Prayerful Forgiveness

How do you forgive? This book offers many solutions, but our favorite method is through praying for help. To forgive the unforgivable, you need a power greater than your own. You need God's unlimited wisdom and unconditional love.

After all, harboring judgment toward another affects your own self-view. If you see yourself as being "damaged" or identify yourself as an "abuse survivor," then you won't recognize yourself as the Divinely perfect, whole, and complete person whom God created. Letting go of judgment is the greatest favor you can do for yourself, with the added benefit of your children having a happier and healthier parent themselves.

In truth, only someone who is already hurt can hurt others. It is very likely that your father experienced hurt as a child from *his* father or mother. As we've said repeatedly, this does not excuse his abusive behavior, of course, but it may explain it.

Perhaps your father found that he could not express love in the way you craved and needed as a child because he was never shown that love himself. As we discussed earlier, the previous generations of fathers (1930s through 1970s) were often disengaged and not as involved with their children as the current ones (1980s, 1990s, 2000s).

The pattern of social conditioning of men is changing. Men are evolving and are increasingly getting in touch with their emotions.

Knowing this may not actually help you if you suffered as a result of having a father from a previous generation. In fact, you may be feeling envious at seeing younger dads engage in a loving way with their children.

Forgiving yourself and forgiving your father is the way out of this hell of continuous anger and resentment.

June felt close to God and the angels throughout her childhood. She always knew there was a God. She enjoyed the company of angels and fairies right up until her preteen years. Her parents accepted her spiritual side. One day when June was around 12, she tragically lost her father, who had been unconditionally loving and accepting toward her. She found that after this event, she lost her faith in God.

She could no longer hear and see the angels or feel their presence. She felt abandoned and betrayed by God. It was as though her grief and trauma caused her pipeline to Heaven to close.

After a period of grieving and processing her feelings and working with a spiritual advisor as a young adult, June found that she could trust God and herself again. She learned that she needed to forgive her father for abandoning her. When she forgave her earthly father, her connection with her Heavenly Father was reestablished.

Here is a helpful prayer for forgiveness:

"Dear God, I am leaning upon Your strength and power to increase my own sense of strength and power. I need Your help,

*please, in healing my heart and mind from anger and sadness
about my father. Please help me to know that You are my
true Father, so that I can access the paternal love that I crave
through You. Please help me to purge myself of toxic resentment
or grudges. Help me to not take my father's actions personally,
but rather to know that he was incapable of giving me love and
care. I pray for a healing miracle of forgiveness."*

Writing a Letter to Your Father

This is a technique that is especially useful when you first
uncover the father wound and you have things you need to get
off your chest and express to him. You might also be in a position
where you cannot openly talk to your father about the impact that
either his absence or actions had upon you.

Andrew: If your father is like mine, he may not actually
know how to handle conversations about emotions. When I have
tried to have those heart-to-heart talks with my father, he didn't
respond in an empathetic manner. Basically he was dismissive of
my concerns and feelings. That can be hurtful, so this is where
writing a letter can help.

In a letter that you won't send, pour out your heart about the
loss, sense of unfairness, betrayal, anger, and rage that you have
felt. Allow the impact of your father wound to be fully expressed.
You can write down how you feel about the fact that the same
pattern of betrayal has occurred throughout your life. You may
feel cheated out of having a happy life and happy relationships.

As you write, you may feel a sense of guilt that you are bringing up these grievances and painful experiences. Many of us have
been conditioned not to "air our dirty laundry," or perhaps you
grew up in a family in which a lot of things were swept under
the carpet.

Well, this exercise is like doing mental and emotional house-cleaning or clearing. The guilt you may feel is natural. You may have been told that you must respect your parents, so speaking or writing about your pain may actually be breaking family rules.

You can still write a modified form of the letter and send it if you feel that is appropriate. Please don't put yourself at risk either emotionally or physically if you believe there may be ramifications at all. In truth, writing the letter and burning it safely or burying it is a powerful gesture or ritual in and of itself. It can help to unburden you of all that buildup of feelings that you may have been carrying around for a very long time.

HEALING SELF-ANGER

Guilt is a form of anger directed toward yourself. If you blame yourself for the original abuse or abandonment (as many children do), you may unconsciously continue to feel guilty into adulthood. Children blame themselves for all sorts of things that they had no control over. Often, this guilt is so deeply lodged that you're not aware of it except for its symptoms of low self-esteem and a tendency to sabotage yourself.

Forgiving yourself may sound strange; however, as we discussed in Chapter 1, a child doesn't understand what may have occurred when they were a little boy or girl. You may have blamed yourself for your parents arguing and divorcing. In some strange way, you may feel that it was your fault if you were abused or mistreated. It is a natural response of a child to sometimes take on the hurt that actually belongs to the parent.

Realizing that you may have taken on parental pain and forgiving yourself for having done so is of paramount importance. You can simply say over and over to your inner child, "You've done nothing wrong. You are not at fault here. You did the best that you could to get through this experience." You can reassure your inner child that you can take it from here and that you the adult can now keep yourself safe.

Abuse is never the fault of the child! No matter how twisted the excuse was from the abuser, there is no circumstance in which a child "deserves" the infliction of pain. Parenthood does not give anyone the right to hurt another person physically or emotionally. Parenting is about loving, protecting, nurturing, and guiding the child.

Doreen: In my clinical psychology experience, children who were sexually abused had confused images of themselves. Many times, the sexual abuse experience was the only time that the child received attention from the abuser. And the child was so love-starved that she was coerced into sexual abuse out of desperation for Dad's approval or a feeling of specialness.

Later, there was self-loathing because the child knew that the sexual abuse was unhealthy, and guilt for "cheating" on Mom and being the "other woman." When sexual abuse survivors admit these secret feelings to themselves, a huge burden is lifted from them. They realize that they were not old enough to have consensual sexual relations with anyone, let alone a father figure. This realization is often followed by rage toward the abuser and the silent parent who didn't protect or intervene (usually the mother).

In adulthood, guilt may arise because of difficult choices you've had to make. For example, if you've chosen not to see your father because of his ongoing abusiveness, you may still harbor guilt. Or you may secretly blame yourself for not being able to "get over it," even though intellectually you know that no one should cope with abuse.

Unblocking or releasing shame can be a powerful way of healing from father wounds if the shame, guilt, and fear were connected to not having loving and safe experiences with your father.

Bianca was abused by many men, including her father, from a young age. She felt consumed by guilt and shame even though nothing that happened to her was her fault. She could no longer trust men and found it hard to identify with male figures like Jesus.

Instead, Bianca loved to read about the Divine sacred feminine energy, such as goddesses and angels. She particularly loved the female archangel Ariel, whose name means "Lioness of God." By learning to call on this angel of feminine strength and power, she regained her own inner strength and courage.

Bianca also read books about Mother Mary. She was not Catholic, but she loved looking at icons of her. Bianca knew that Mother Mary was there for everyone, regardless of their religious background, and she received beautiful nurturing energy whenever she called on her. One night, after she said prayers and lit candles, she sensed Mother Mary's presence. Bianca could feel Mother Mary put her arm around her and drape her blue veil over her head and heart. She sobbed for a while, feeling years of shame, guilt, and pain wash away and a deep sense of release.

Mother Mary, who is sometimes called the rose without thorns, had healed Bianca's soul of grief, shame, and despair. She felt her heart open again, knowing that she could protect herself with her Divine feminine power. Bianca now regularly wears rose oil, and her heart swells each time she is reminded of Mother Mary's love.

☒ ☒ ☒

We are here to learn lessons and to resolve old conflicts in a peaceful way. That doesn't mean you become friends with your abuser. It does mean that you find some peace of mind through forgiveness and Divine grace. That is our prayer and the intention of this book. Carrying the pain, anger, and suffering of an abusive childhood really does weigh you down. The intention of this book is to help you find your freedom and live a life without burdens.

☒ ☒ ☒ ☒ ☒

Chapter Nine

Accepting Your Feelings through Mindfulness

When you feel unpleasant emotions like loss, jealousy, rage, rejection, and any other range of emotional states, it's important to know that they aren't permanent. They are signs from your deeper self that are trying to gain your attention, and they are encouraging you to make positive changes and move toward healing.

Mindfulness is one of the techniques from the Buddhist tradition that can help with simply being present with what is happening for you and not escaping or avoiding these emotions. There is a part of your mind that is an observer. It sits within the mind and yet is part of the larger, more expansive part of your higher self or soul. It is the wise and somewhat neutral part of you that you can access with gentle processing and breathing, such as simply asking yourself, *Who is feeling this?*

This aspect of you is called the *wise mind*. It is aware of emotions and simply acknowledges them like clouds passing through the sky. It is actually a very vast space or awareness that sits between your emotional self and your intellectual self. It can be a place you feel either in your heart or your mind. Once you access that part of yourself, you don't become attached to what you are feeling, and you are less impacted by your emotions.

There are many books on mindfulness that you can refer to. This chapter is merely an introduction.

CALMING AND GROUNDING YOURSELF

You can be the observer of your feelings rather than being swamped by them. Simply accept them; don't judge them.

Allow the feeling to flow through you. It often dissipates by itself. Please try to name the feeling and bring that feeling into your left brain by saying things like:

- "This feeling of distress is from my childhood experiences."
- "I acknowledge that my past was difficult."
- "I can accept and cope with this feeling."
- "I know this feeling is temporary."
- "There is much more to me than my feelings."

Present-Moment Awareness

Bring yourself into the present moment. Carry a crystal or a talisman (an object that has special meaning to you). This can also be a book, a crucifix, a bottle of holy water or oil, or anything else that brings you comfort when you touch or hold it. If you have a pet, playing with an animal can bring you back into the present moment as well.

Other ways of putting yourself in the present moment are to carefully and lovingly bring your awareness back into your body, feeling yourself positioned in the chair you are sitting on, and your feet solidly on the floor. Bringing your awareness to your feet and imagining roots running from your feet deep into the earth can prevent you from overly intellectualizing, and put you more in your heart space. It relieves any "static" or "energy charge" that you may be feeling. The earth lovingly accepts this energy, and you may feel the planet's energy reciprocate, sending you love. *You* can also reciprocate by caretaking for the planet through eco-friendly practices.

Self-Soothing

Self-soothing is another technique. You may feel as though you don't deserve pleasure in your life, or you may feel guilty or unworthy of enjoying your life. Our father wound can mean that we overlook seeing the beauty in everyday life. Self-soothing is a technique from a psychological therapy called *dialectical behavioral therapy.*

Part of this therapy involves bringing yourself into the present moment, appreciating or improving the present moment. There are a range of techniques involved with this therapy that you may find useful. Some of the strategies may sound familiar. These include saying calming and reassuring things to yourself such as "This feeling will pass," or "I choose peace instead of this."

Some techniques can involve really simple activities involving your five senses that reduce those uncomfortable feelings and bring you into the present moment, such as listening to uplifting music or playing a musical instrument. Music that you find relaxing or inspiring can change your mood quickly. Singing along can engage your being as well. It doesn't matter what you sound like. It's about the good mood that singing, listening to, or playing a tune can bring you. If you feel shy or embarrassed, you can close your doors and windows so you can sing loudly without worrying what others may think if they hear you.

Pleasurable Smells

Smells, including oils, stimulate the part of the brain that involves your emotions. Using pure essential oils—including orange, ylang-ylang, and rose—can help uplift you. Choose a calming scent such as lavender if you are feeling stressed. You don't need an oil burner or diffuser; simply smelling from a bottle or spraying some oil on a tissue or under your pillow can settle your mood quickly.

Cooking comforting food can also be a calming activity that brings a warming, nourishing smell to your home. Just be honest with yourself if you begin binge eating, which is a sign of emotional discomfort. The 12-step program Overeaters Anonymous and/or working with a therapist trained in eating disorder counseling can be helpful in breaking this pattern.

Walk into a forest. Inhale those rich, earthy smells. The smell of the ocean instantly calms and refreshes you too, as does being near water.

Exciting the Eyes

If we are feeling wounded, unworthy, or depressed, we may not see the beauty that is actually present in our lives every day. Finding and appreciating it can uplift your mood and can fill you with a sense of gratitude for the Creator and for life in general.

Appreciating beauty in the form of art and music isn't something that is restricted to "special people" or the privileged few. Paintings, sculpture, and installations are available for everyone to view. It costs nothing to wander through some local art galleries. Even many private ones are open to the public. You can wander around and fill your vision with art that inspires and uplifts. We do suggest keeping away from exhibitions that focus on the dark side of life or the macabre.

Aside from that, wandering through your local botanical gardens and appreciating the flowering plants, trees, and shrubs of all different varieties can fill you with wonder and reverence.

Watching butterflies, bees, or waterbirds such as ducks and swans can also bring you peace and relaxation, especially when you observe them mindfully and see how they don't struggle or stress. Most of the time they appear to be relaxed in the present moment and live life without effort.

The Power of Prayer

Prayer is another way of accessing something vaster than you and your father wound. It is also a fundamental component of the healing within 12-step programs. Prayer is profound and can bring instant healing from deep-seated emotions. It is about surrendering to the mystical healing power of the Infinite.

Doreen: I have had personal and professional experiences of prayer completely eliminating addictive cravings. Years ago I had strong daily cravings for wine, coffee, and chocolate. I had no choice but to partake, so they were no longer pleasant indulgences. They were leaving me bloated, hungover, and with headaches. So, I prayed intently to be released from my addictions. I was completely open to a healing, and wasn't hanging on to any control or desire for the addictions. The next day after my fervent prayer, I no longer craved the wine, coffee, and chocolate I had been addicted to. To me, it was a miracle to be released from the cravings! I still don't partake of these addictive substances, and I don't crave them either.

I've also received hundreds of testimonies from people who've been released from addictive cravings after they prayed for help. It's not a special prayer that creates the healing; rather, it's the action of humbly and sincerely asking for and accepting God's help.

Studies show that prayer has a healing effect upon addictions. For example, *ScienceDaily* magazine reported on May 12, 2016, that the prayers recited by members of Alcoholics Anonymous resulted in measurable reductions in cravings for alcohol:

In the first study to explore brain physiology in AA members, researchers from NYU Langone Medical Center found that members who recited AA prayers after viewing drinking-related images reported less craving for alcohol after praying than after just reading a newspaper. The reduced craving in those that prayed corresponded to increased activity in brain regions responsible for attention and emotion as measured by MRI, according to study results published recently in the *American Journal of Drug and Alcohol Abuse.*

"Our findings suggest that the experience of AA over the years had left these members with an innate ability to use the AA experience—prayer in this case—to minimize the effect of alcohol triggers in producing craving," says senior author Marc Galanter, MD, Professor of Psychiatry and Director of the Division of Alcoholism and Drug Abuse at NYU Langone. "Craving is diminished in long-term AA members compared to patients who have stopped drinking for some period of time but are more vulnerable to relapse."

The *form* of the prayer isn't as important as you being *sincere* and open to a healing. If some part of you is a rebel who fears being controlled by God, you won't be as open to receiving a healing. You must truly be ready to be freed of addictions, and then your prayer will be answered.

Without addictions to numb the pain, the wounded inner child can seem loud and difficult to handle. That's why having emotional support from prayer, a counselor, or a 12-step sponsor is essential. You may also need to change your social circle if your friends' partying could lead you to relapse. Choosing healthy friendships is part of the path of healing from father wounds.

Unifying your will through Divine will and praying to God, Holy Spirit, Jesus, and the angels for healing your mind and emotions can be profound. As in the 12-step program, you realize that connecting to something bigger than yourself or your higher self can be empowering in itself. Prayer connects you to that universal power and energy, and you no longer feel alone in your suffering and your grief.

If this sounds a little too religious, know that some people prefer not to use the word *God* and may substitute *Universe* or *Higher Power*. Please use whatever words make you feel comfortable. However, be honest if you're using these synonyms because of a dislike or distrust of male energy. This is a sign of needing to heal father wounds so that you can benefit from the blessings that come from both Divine Feminine *and* Masculine energies.

Restorative and Gentle Yoga

Doreen: As I wrote about in my book *Don't Let Anything Dull Your Sparkle,* research shows that gentle and restorative yoga can significantly reduce your body's stress levels and post-traumatic symptoms. Stress hormones are reduced, and there's a more peaceful outlook following a session.

Yoga must be *gentle* or *restorative* in order to having this healing effect:

- **Gentle yoga** involves yoga poses that are easier and less strenuous, with a slower flow from one pose to the other. Teachers generally speak in soft, gentle voices, and the music is meditative.

- **Restorative yoga** refers to holding yoga poses for up to ten minutes, often with the aid of yoga straps. This allows the muscle memory to release pent-up emotional energies.

Some yoga studios use the term *yin yoga* instead of the term *gentle* or *restorative yoga.*

Research shows that while more active and strenuous forms of yoga do achieve fitness goals, they can also increase stress hormones. This is especially true if there is a competitive nature to the class, such as comparing yourself to other students, fast-paced music, or shame when the teacher corrects your poses.

Nearly every yoga studio offers gentle, yin, and restorative classes. Do make sure that the teacher of the class isn't a substitute, however. I have found that substitute teachers who normally teach advanced yoga classes often impose their faster, more competitive styles upon students of gentle classes.

You can also find wonderful classes for free on YouTube, and through paid subscriptions to Gaia.com. There are also Christian yoga classes called "Holy Yoga," which offer inspiring Bible verses for each pose, and also "Laughter Yoga," in which you enjoy belly laughs with your yoga class.

Just be sure to do yoga poses safely, and don't push yourself to do anything painful. If you have physical limitations, please talk to your doctor before doing yoga.

If you can afford it, we recommend hiring a gentle teacher from your local yoga studio to give you private instruction. Or, you and your friends can split the cost. Private instruction helps you safely practice yoga with gentle supervision.

Yoga is a quick stress-reducing method. It can be as simple as putting a large towel on the floor, lying on your back, stretching, and rolling from side to side.

Salt Baths

Salt is a natural detoxifier, especially when mixed into warm water to speed up its molecular activity. So, soaking in a warm bath filled with salt is relaxing and purifying to the body and energy.

If you tend to absorb other people's energies, then salt baths can clear away negativity that you may be storing. *Empaths* are those of us who can feel everyone's emotions, and we often mistake these feelings for our own.

Soaking in a warm salt bath helps you reset yourself to the person whom God created as peaceful, joyful, and loving.

We recommend using sea salt that you purchase in the spice section of health-food stores, or buy it online. You can add your own essential oils, and place candles around the perimeter of your bathtub for a relaxing, spa-like ambience. Play some meditation music to give your salt bath an extra therapeutic benefit.

If you don't have a bathtub, you can mix warm water and salt to make a clay-like texture. Then place this mixture on your chest so that it covers your heart, to draw out painful emotions If you have sensitive skin, we recommend doing this in the shower so you can quickly wash off the salt.

Once you detox and release pent-up emotions, it's essential to fill up the vacant space with positivity. The best and easiest way to do so is to pray: *"Dear God, please fill me up completely with Your pure healing love."* You'll feel the positive shift, and will rest easy knowing that you're now super-shielded inside and out.

Dream Work and Dream Journaling

Dreams, and processing information while you are asleep, are effective ways of healing yourself from father issues and other challenges.

When you sleep, your body and your ego are also resting, which means that you can more easily connect with the higher realms of God, Holy Spirit, Jesus, your higher self, and the angels for healing and guidance.

As you're falling asleep, you can ask for help, healing, and insights into your father issues. Holy Spirit (the great teacher of God's wisdom) and your guardian angels, especially the guardian angel who is your "Dream Guide," will help you to conduct deep emotional healing and gain understanding during your dream time. When you wake up, you may not remember everything that was conveyed in your dreams. However, you'll still benefit from the experience.

Keep a dream journal by your bedside to record your dreams as soon as you wake up. Some dreams are a form of clearing your mind.

Andrew: One of my clients saw herself standing up to her father in her dream. It was as though the dream was a "dress rehearsal" for when she literally had to do that in her life.

Soon after, she was feeling troubled and upset after visiting her father. She had possibly absorbed some of his emotional and physical pain when she went to visit him.

That night, she asked her Dream Guide and angels to please clear this pain from her body and mind. It was as simple as that. She woke up refreshed and free from the emotional pain she'd been carrying.

Breath Work

Another way of accessing this mindful space is through your breath. Use diaphragmatic breathing, or deep breathing from your abdomen, to instantly bring a sense of calm.

Simply focus on the in breath, and you can say to yourself, *I breathe in peace*; and as you exhale, you can say inwardly, *I breathe out fear.* Once you do this a few times, your emotions will calm down. If thoughts and emotions come in, simply acknowledge them and accept them and bring your attention back to your breath.

This is one of the simplest ways of bringing calm to yourself. It is effective for conditions such as anxiety and depression as well. Once you are feeling calm and centered, it is much easier to connect with that wise mind, the calm observer you have within. You can feel your own being or essence, which can bring healing because the emotions that once dominated lose their grip, and you realize that you are much vaster than those emotions. That leads to a sense of feeling empowered rather than victimized by your emotions.

✂ ✂ ✂ ✂ ✂

Chapter Ten

WOUNDED-CHILD
THERAPY

Working with your inner child is an important step toward recovery and healing from a difficult childhood. Emotional pain as a result of your father or other males putting you down and not treating you well can affect your subconscious mind. As a child, you couldn't process an angry adult's intentions. At that time, you didn't have the capacity to protect yourself and assert your needs.

If you have felt violated physically, sexually, emotionally, or mentally, it's likely that a part of you felt rage, terror, powerlessness, and a sense of betrayal and vulnerability. Just as you couldn't understand adult anger, you could not—and did not know how to—process and deal with your own strong emotions. As a result, they stayed deep within your subconscious mind.

As a child, you wanted love and approval, *and* you wanted to survive. It wasn't safe to express your emotions when you were very young, so you may have suppressed them. You probably felt anxiety, which may have presented as compulsive or repetitive behavior. You may have regressed and become clingy. Bed-wetting can be another sign that you were anxious as a child.

Childhood is such a critical time, and you were *meant* to feel safe, secure, protected, and loved. We seem to know this intrinsic truth. If you didn't experience this, you may have felt traumatized.

Please don't invalidate your feelings by saying to yourself, *Oh, my childhood wasn't that bad,* or *I know other people had it much worse.* This is called *minimizing,* which is a form of the denial defense mechanism. Minimizing is an attempt to make things seem less significant than they really are.

Rather than minimizing your past, the intention of doing inner-child work is to heal and transmute the pain you have experienced.

MEETING THE INNER CHILD

We've talked about an inner child or wounded child at several points in this book—but what exactly *is* this?

In simple terms, it is a part of your subconscious mind. It seems to have a life of its own. Some people describe it as a subpersonality or another aspect of yourself. Of course there is not a literal child inside you; however, there *is* a part of your mind that is still caught up in the drama and chaos and pain of your childhood.

Through this powerful work, the inner child or wounded child will no longer run the ship. You will feel more at peace and in control of your emotions and behavior. The child within you most of all wants to know that you are not going to abandon them—that you will be there to protect and nurture them.

Please note: Working with your inner child is intense. The child within may experience raw and very primal emotions that were long left unexpressed. Repressed memories, with strong unhealed emotions, may come flooding out. If you are feeling particularly vulnerable and unsettled, we would suggest that you don't do these exercises alone. They can be done with a therapist or counselor who is familiar with this work.

Bringing strong emotions such as rage and anger to the surface can be unsettling, because often we're not accustomed to feeling them. We may have judged these emotions, or been punished for expressing emotions in childhood, and so suppressed them for a lifetime.

If the emotions that this exercise brings up are too intense, then slow the process down and take a break for a few days before resuming accessing or dialoguing with your inner child.

There is now increasing evidence to show that working with your wounded child is effective and actually "rewires" the brain. It is a way of receiving the nurturing that your parents were probably unable to give you at the time, because they didn't know how to or were wounded themselves.

If memories of forgotten abuse begin to surface, it's best to have regular appointments with a counselor or attend a free Emotions Anonymous meeting (EmotionsAnonymous.org) to get emotional support. Once again, the purpose of this work is not to create or re-create more drama or to relive the trauma. The intention is to express and release long-held emotions.

If you do remember an abuse scenario, you may not know how to handle your changed perspective on this relationship. Avoid the impulse to confront the abuser until you've had time to gain strength. Many abusers, when confronted by the person they abused, deny it. The abuser is often so racked with guilt that they cannot face what they did. Of course, after they pass from the earth, they will understand the gravity of their hurtful behavior. Until then, though, many abusers continue to deny that they actually abused anyone.

In your fantasy, your abuser will apologize and become the ideal father. This is rarely what occurs, though, unfortunately. Many abusers committed their actions while in an alcoholic blackout or while out of their minds due to drug use or a psychotic episode, so they actually may not remember the incident.

That's why it's important to wait and see if confrontation is the best method for you. We recommend focusing upon healing yourself rather than punishing the person who abused you.

Remember that you don't need to do this alone. It is actually advisable to seek out a therapist or counselor for support. If a traumatic memory surfaces, you may need qualified support to deal with it, such as a crisis hotline or a therapist trained in trauma recovery (the website emdr.com has lists of therapists worldwide).

If you ever feel like harming yourself, please immediately call a crisis hotline, or seek help from mental health services, which can support you in finding other ways of managing painful feelings and soothing yourself. This book also contains some of these strategies.

STEPS TO HEALING THE INNER CHILD

Doing these inner child exercises is a great addition or complement to any counseling or therapy that you may already be engaged in.

1. Access your inner child. Start by asking your inner child, *How are you feeling right now? What would you like me to know?* It may help to have a photograph of yourself as a child beside you. You can make the space where you do this exercise inviting to your inner child by placing toys, teddy bears, or a children's blanket or night-light next to you.

2. Gain your inner child's trust. In truth, that part of you may have felt abandoned, betrayed, neglected, and forgotten by you, the adult self. You may need to take a little time to gain the trust of that part of your child self.

Much like you would in a conversation with a friend who is feeling vulnerable, reassure your child that it's safe to communicate. At first your inner child may feel that they cannot trust you because they felt ignored or suppressed for so long. Reassuring the child (yourself) that you are now there for them will help the child feel safe. It's important that your inner child trusts your willingness to listen to, feel, see, or otherwise sense what they are experiencing.

3. Allow yourself to feel your inner child's feelings. Allow all of your feelings to rise to the surface. You may be surprised by what comes up when you first decide to say hello to that part of yourself. Expressing with the intention of releasing is so therapeutic. There will probably be tears of sadness, hurt, shame, and anger. Crying is always a good release, and in a short while, you'll start feeling more compassionate toward yourself.

You may feel afraid that if you unleash your anger, you'll lose control. You won't. In fact, you'll have more control once you release the built-up energy of suppressed emotions. Without an outlet, those buried feelings always bubble up in ways that aren't pretty, so it's important to unearth them. Your unconscious mind won't give you more than you can handle.

Commit to doing this exercise weekly. Doing so establishes trust with the lost and abandoned aspects of yourself. Your child within begins to trust you. Your inner child begins to feel heard and understood. Make a commitment that you will never abandon yourself. That is a promise that you need to keep with yourself—that is, to take great care of yourself and your inner child.

During the initial stages of this exercise, it can be intense, so please go gently throughout the whole process and don't try to force anything to happen. There is an aspect of Divine timing with all of this.

Automatic Writing

One of the ways that you can access the inner child is through drawing and writing with your nondominant hand (the hand you normally don't write with). Doing this bypasses your conscious mind to access layers of your psyche that you normally aren't aware of.

You may get a symbol, a word, or sentences. Your writing will look messy and may appear childlike. You may be surprised by what comes from your subconscious mind and what you may have repressed. Don't be afraid of or censor angry words or images that may come to the surface. Just allow any figure, shape, or drawing to appear. They are symbols for the rage that a part of you experienced and later "forgot" or suppressed. Just let the images flow out onto the page.

Andrew: I remember when I first did this exercise, I was surprised by the somewhat violent image that I drew, which came from repressed anger. This method was needed so it could be released.

After doing this inner-child exercise a few times, you may notice that you and your inner child begin to feel lighter and that you've established trust in the process. Your inner child will appear happier, and your communication will be friendlier without the edge of anger or sarcasm that you may have previously expressed. This means that you are on your way toward healing.

You will notice a sense of calmness and peace that perhaps you haven't felt in a long time. It's as though the angst, anger, hurt, and fear no longer lurk in your subconscious and have been safely discharged.

You may find that spontaneously any addictive patterns and behavior will naturally subside. The reason for your addiction in the first place becomes clear, and you no longer have a need or desire to block out the pain through using food or drugs.

REWARDING YOUR INNER CHILD

If you feel like your inner child is sulking or doesn't want to interact, promise them (yourself) that you will "treat" them afterward. Make sure that you follow through, and after doing this exercise, find a fun activity to do together.

The following are a few ideas to reward your inner child for cooperating with you:

- Color in coloring books. They are becoming popular destressing tools for adults and are available in most bookstores. Several coloring books featuring angels, fairies, mermaids, and unicorns are published by Hay House. As you gently color, do so mindfully and simply enjoy the activity for what it is.

- Make your inner child a card. Write a loving message in the card and decorate it with glitter, stickers, and colorful pictures.

- Go outside and play. Finding a peaceful park with swings can be fun! Please take due care that the swing set supports adults, and don't worry about what others think. Or, if you prefer to stay in the privacy of your own home, make a fort out of blankets that you hang over chairs in your living room.

- Watch a fun children's movie that will gladden your heart (and your child self), such as your favorite film from childhood.

- Treat your inner child to a sweet or favorite food to awaken positive feelings.

- Play with a toy, doll, or teddy bear to amuse your inner child.

You might feel silly doing some of these things. Please choose a quiet setting by yourself so that you aren't concerned with other people's judgments.

Other activities you can do as an adult that engage the child self are:

- Organize a costume party with your friends or play dress-up with children. Many communities have groups dedicated to costume play, including cosplay groups, the Society for Creative Anachronism, Renaissance festivals, live-action role-playing gatherings, mermaid swim groups, and fairy parties.

- Join a drama club or an improvisation theater group. Playacting different characters stimulates your imagination. For the purpose of this exercise, choose one that is lighthearted and allows for silliness.

- Play fun board games and noncompetitive sports. Generally goofing around can awaken your childlike spirit and invigorate your energy.

- Buy yourself a stuffed animal to hug.

WORKING WITH YOUR WOUNDED ADOLESCENT

You may be thinking, *Aren't we done yet with talking to our inner self?* The reality is that dialoguing with different parts of yourself, such as your inner child and adolescent, can be a process that continues throughout your life.

The upside is that it gets much easier, and you can simply do a quick check-in with your child self and ask them what they would like today. Often it is just a reassurance or a promise to follow through and have more fun and play in your life. Make sure that you keep that promise to yourself.

Your inner adolescent is a natural extension of your inner child. Your child self *does* mature into an adolescent or teenager.

What were your teens like? Where you depressed, lonely, or anxious? Did you act out your anger or confusion? What type of friends did you attract? Did you engage in substance abuse?

The chances are that if you didn't have a loving father figure in your life, you may have had issues with confidence, assertiveness, and self-esteem. Trauma underlies many psychological issues, so working with these wounded aspects of yourself can be beneficial for finding peace of mind. Truthfully, you may have benefited from counseling as a teen, and if you didn't receive proper emotional support then, our compassion is with you. And it's never too late to heal your teenage heart.

It's therapeutic to reflect upon your childhood and adolescence, and think of the times when you experienced a significant loss, trauma, or change. When these memories arise, reassure your inner child or adolescent that the mature adult is now providing love and protection.

The wounded adolescent and child are parts of you that became "frozen" with fear and shock when you were abused or abandoned at that age. If you experienced a big trauma in childhood, you may be "emotionally frozen" at a certain point. Although you've matured physically into an adult, emotionally you feel stuck at the age where you suffered severe hurt.

It's important to spend time with the wounded child or adolescent at each age, as all are craving attention, reassurance, and nurturing. *You* are the best person to provide what you need at every stage.

Andrew: I know that when I did this inner-child exercise, I uncovered that part of me that felt sad and didn't fit in. I felt shame about who I was in terms of my sexuality, and I didn't have the knowledge or the skills to reconcile who I was with the religion I grew up in. This left my adolescent self feeling vulnerable and inadequate.

I believe that these aspects of myself could be picked up on by others who perhaps wanted to exploit my weaknesses in relationships. This was a tough learning experience for me.

It is worth doing this exploration, no matter how troubling it may be. The destructive power of memories and feelings exists only when they are repressed. Once exposed to the daylight of conscious awareness, these repressed memories and feelings have much less power over you. Your adult self takes charge instead of you being ruled by a wounded inner youth.

How is your inner adolescent currently feeling? You may want to look at your high school photos and check in with that inner teenage boy or girl. How are they feeling? What would they want you to know? You are likely to experience strong feelings, and you probably want to give your inner adolescent equally strong messages, such as:

Don't worry—your life will improve, and I will look after you. The things that are troubling you now won't bother you as much as you mature. You are resilient, and you can stand up for yourself. Please focus upon what you are good at and give yourself a break. You don't have to work it all out at once. Your life will make more sense as you mature, and you will learn to accept and love the parts of you that you feel ashamed of.

Having a two-way conversation with your inner teenager can help you to accept and love yourself more. This method can lead you to have a peaceful appreciation for yourself.

Shame

Shame is one of those toxic emotions that springs from childhood and continues into your adolescence, especially if there were secrets or deep wounds that weren't dealt with. The difference between shame and guilt is that shame is feeling bad about yourself, while guilt is feeling bad about an action.

You may even feel that somehow you deserved or caused some of the painful experiences in your life. Spiritually, you may have entered into a soul agreement to experience some of the things that happened to you; however, the human part of you may not be aware of that.

The child in you may feel guilty and afraid, and the adolescent (unless they receive in-depth counseling) may try to cover up those feelings, which can then lie dormant within you and may be experienced as shame.

What we want to emphasize to you is this: feeling ashamed doesn't mean that there's something to feel ashamed about.

The fact that your father couldn't love you enough has to do with him, and isn't a reflection of your lovability. His heart was closed to love, and you could have been the world's perfect child but he still was incapable of loving you in the way that you needed.

Simply accepting these truths and emotions can be beneficial. Tell your inner adolescent that it's okay to experience whatever they may be feeling about the events in their past—regrets about things they may have done, or lies told—as well as about themselves, their body, or their sexuality.

Bringing compassion to yourself, your emotions, and your wounds can greatly alleviate those feelings that may have been covered up through years of addiction, self-harm, overeating, or simply feeling bad about yourself.

Repressed Emotions

Andrew: During the course of writing this book, my stepfather became very ill. In addition, I found out that my biological father's health was failing as well.

These events triggered a grief for the relationship that I never had with either of them. I found myself experiencing the same feelings I did as an adolescent.

I thought that with my father figures being unwell, they'd somehow become kinder and more compassionate. What I found was that I *was* able to have more meaningful conversations with them, yet with a couple of thoughtless comments from one of them, I was plunged into a well of sadness and pain that I hadn't felt since I was a teen.

It seemed that my inner adolescent's wounds were coming to the surface. It was tempting to quell those feelings with overeating, numbing, and watching TV excessively. I found there weren't enough carbohydrates in the world to stem the tide of pain that was rising up for healing.

Finally, I just allowed the tears to flow. As I simply sat with my feelings and felt them fully, the pain began to ebb.

What might easily have been diagnosed as depression was in fact deeply held feelings that needed to be expressed. After several days of crying, I felt better.

One of the other things that I found helpful was to pray for healing and for peace to be restored as I went to sleep. A lot of healing occurs while you're sleeping, and getting good sleep helped me enormously during this time, as did finding an herbal supplement to boost serotonin naturally. Sunshine and exercise can do the same thing. (If you find yourself oversleeping, though, and not wanting to get out of bed, this can be a sign of clinical depression that needs a therapist's support.)

After allowing my emotions to flow freely, I was able to be present with my inner adolescent. I discovered that what he needed was compassion and understanding. I began to have an honest dialogue with my inner wounded adolescent and asked him what he wanted. Instantly I felt that all he wanted was to be acknowledged and heard.

I remember pushing my feelings down as an adolescent, frightened of the sorrow that I felt. I thought that the sadness and depression would never end.

Most of us weren't taught how to manage our emotions, or how to simply feel them and allow them to flow through us. So, we ignored them, suppressed them, or expressed them inappropriately.

Doreen: In my family, we were told "Don't rock the boat" and "Try to remain calm" whenever my brother, Ken, and I were upset. Both my mom and my dad had alcoholic parents who loudly and dramatically argued all the time. So my parents felt unsafe around strong emotions, which reminded them of their drama-filled childhoods.

My brother and I both learned to repress anger and sadness, instead of expressing them. When I was taking undergraduate psychology courses, one of my professors asked all us students to pose the question "How am I feeling right now?" My answers were all intellectually based, such as "I'm feeling tired" or "I'm bored." My professor worked with me to help me understand and experience emotions with my heart and body, not my mind.

He gave us a chart with cartoon faces showing different expressions (similar to emojis) that named dozens of emotions. That chart and my professor helped me to notice, acknowledge, understand, and process my repressed emotions. It was a gentle and peaceful experience that helped me to be a person today who is very aware and appreciative of the rainbow of different emotions that we all feel. I also learned how to deal with conflict in healthy, honest ways (a topic I wrote about in *Assertiveness for Earth Angels*).

Accessing your inner adolescent as part of your work with your inner child can be powerful and transformative.

Once you have felt and expressed the sadness, hurt, humiliation, and anger, you can more consciously and easily connect with your inner peace and calm. Happier emotions are more freely felt and expressed.

Chapter Eleven

※ ※ ※ ※ ※

REPARENTING YOURSELF:

Reimagining Your Childhood and Life Story

After you have connected with your inner child and have expressed and explored the pain, hurt, anger, and grief, then you can gently and lovingly provide your inner child with whatever you were lacking when you were small and powerless.

In some cases, it may not be possible to reconcile with your father and have the type of relationship that you'd like with him. Maybe his heart is closed, or he's actively alcoholic, or he simply cannot express his love and appreciation for you. Perhaps he's afraid of feeling strong emotions, or he's terrified of facing his feelings of guilt. So where does that leave you? Fortunately, there are ways that you can, as an adult, reparent yourself.

In addition to the voice of our inner child, we already have a wise and loving adult part of us that is ready, willing, and able to take care of the wounded aspect of ourselves.

In spiritual truth, we are already healed. Within the wider metaphysical view, the ultimate truth of who you are is already healed and whole. God created you perfect, whole, and complete; and that hasn't changed. The purpose of this book is to help you to reach that awareness of your Divine perfection.

It is tempting to make excuses to avoid getting in touch with your pain. You might be thinking, *Well, if we are already healed and whole, what is the point of doing these exercises?*

Experiencing the pain and emotional challenges often spur us on toward a new level of spiritual growth and awareness. Our experiences are not meant to disable us or make us so vulnerable that we feel we cannot handle life effectively.

Reparenting yourself and healing the child within can free you from feeling like you're constantly vulnerable. Feeling your feelings and healing them from the vantage point of the wise and loving aspect of yourself can help you to find a sense of peace. From that center within you, you'll no longer feel so afraid and the wounded aspect of yourself will feel more integrated.

Please don't expect a miraculous healing the first time that you do this exercise. At first it might seem somewhat challenging. You will find that each time, it does become easier, and you're able to see the progress that you make. You'll feel lighter, and the child within will begin to feel safe and loved.

So What Does Reparenting Yourself Actually Involve?

Part I of this book acknowledged and explored the impact that father wounds can have on you. The great news is that it's not too late for your inner child to experience the happy childhood that you might have wanted.

If this sounds a little unusual, give yourself some time to ponder and play around with the ideas that are suggested here. They're intended as a self-help guide.

When you do this exercise, it's important to get in touch with the wise and loving parent that you have within you. This is the loving adult self who you really are. In our experience, it's part of the "wise mind" or the observer that sees yourself and your inner child without all the emotion. From this neutral space, the wise inner parent is able to give the inner child all the love, compassion, encouragement, and support that they need.

For example, after your inner child has expressed their hurt and sense of betrayal, you can reassure your inner child with statements such as, "I am here to protect you. I will never allow that to happen again." Visualize yourself at your current age, giving a protective hug to your inner child. If imagining yourself in a parental role triggers you, then see yourself as an elder sibling who teaches, guides, and shields your child self.

Please take a moment right now to breathe and center yourself, and imagine yourself as a child during your times of need. See and feel yourself as an adult stepping into this scene and gently approaching your child self. Allow yourself to sense the fear from your inner child, and reassure your child self of your pure intentions to help with healing, guidance, and protection. You have become your own guardian angel!

You can access that part of you who is wise and loving and is already one with your Divine self or God. Take several deep breaths. Breathe out any tension, fears, and worries.

Try this prayer or something similar from your heart. If the name *God* triggers you, then please substitute with *Creator* or *Source*.

"Dear God, thank You for always loving me unconditionally and completely. Please help me to feel Your love, and to be healed from those times in my life when I didn't feel loved. I ask that You help me to feel whole and complete, and show me the way in which I can also help others to feel Your Divine energy and peacefulness."

You will feel a calm, peaceful, patient, and gender-neutral energy that is the infinite Divine wisdom. This loving energy is your Creator, Who is giving you complete access to all the wisdom, knowledge, and healing that you need to communicate with your inner child and adolescent.

From this expansive space, begin a dialogue with your wounded younger self. You may literally place your arms around yourself and give yourself a hug.

With as much love as you can, reassure and comfort your inner younger self. The messages or communication may sound something like this:

- "It's not your fault."
- "You are a Divinely perfect child of God."
- "You are very loved."
- "Please forgive yourself for any mistakes that you think you've made."
- "You are deserving and worthy of love."
- "Please accept my love."
- "I will never leave you."
- "You are safe and protected now."

This is one method that you can use to reassure yourself that you won't abandon "you." Your inner child may feel betrayed or cheated out of having a happy childhood with loving parents. You learn to soothe those hurt feelings by:

- Singing or humming to yourself.
- Writing a poem or love song to your inner child.
- Rocking yourself gently.
- Playing uplifting, comforting songs, even lullabies.
- Hugging a squishy teddy bear.
- Reminding your inner child that you are "never alone."

You are there now, as the wise, loving adult self to protect and help heal that part of you.

REPLAYING AND REWRITING YOUR CHILDHOOD

Similar to past-life regressions, you can go back in time through visualization and rewrite key incidents of your childhood. You may understandably be skeptical of this idea; however, time is an illusion, and with the help of a hypnotherapist or through meditation, you can go back to the time that an incident occurred and replay it, responding the way you would have liked to have responded. If there is a deep regret that you did or didn't do something, vividly call those incidents to mind and choose to do what you really wanted to do.

Sometimes viewing your life as a play or film can be helpful. Imagine you are sitting in a dark theater. It is warm and comfortable, and you begin to see the story of your relationship with your father unfold on-screen. This time, you are sitting back in a comfortable chair, so some of the sting is taken out of the painful parts of the story, because you are viewing this objectively as an adult.

Of course, if you experienced severe abuse, you will have strong emotional reactions to your memories. If you feel overwhelmed by upsetting feelings, stop the mental movie and step away to process your emotions. Get support if you feel out of control.

Through viewing your childhood as a movie, you're able to see how you internalized and believed what your father or father figures said to you. As a child and adolescent, you didn't have the power of discernment or wisdom to know that your father was acting insanely when he said or did cruel things to you.

You didn't have the ability to process your emotions, and it's possible that you may have "left your body" for periods of time. This is called *dissociation*, a protective mechanism that you used to survive.

Dissociation only becomes a problem if the abused person continues it after the abuse is over. This can lead to a splitting of consciousness, where you feel your entire life is a surreal movie.

A normal example is not remembering how you drove home because you were zoned out. Someone who habitually dissociates won't remember much about their past, because they're perpetually in a spacey trance to guard against potential pain. If you believe you are dissociating habitually, a therapist trained in trauma recovery can help you.

Seeing your inner child self through the eyes of a more mature, wiser, and loving self, you can learn to take charge of your life and destiny. Ultimately, you are the one in charge of this ship of life, *and* you can navigate a new destination for yourself.

For example, if you had a challenging childhood that involved abuse, you can visualize yourself standing up to the perpetrator by saying "No! Leave me alone!" Imagine yourself running to a safe place and protecting yourself.

This can help you to see yourself and your inner child as empowered. It is very reassuring to the inner child to know that they can respond effectively to any future dangers. You are teaching yourself that you can play out scenarios in your life differently. For instance, if you felt like a victim in your past and you replay the scenarios in a more empowered way, then you can more effectively handle incidents as they occur in your present and future.

Your past, present, and future selves are all one. They exist simultaneously in spiritual truth: if you effect change in either the present or the past, you affect your future self.

That doesn't mean that the abuse you suffered as a child did not occur; it means that you're choosing to create another reality that is valid as well.

Often we feel as though our lives are stuck in a continuous loop that brings in the same experiences in a different form. For example, you may feel that you attract the same types of relationships or jobs that replicate your childhood experiences to some degree. Taking this creative approach by visualizing new outcomes can mean that you create new options and alternatives for yourself.

Rewriting the story of your life is very empowering because you get to direct the story lines. If you can imagine the new version of your story with the accompanying happier emotions, your unconscious mind will believe the new version to be true. You can rewire your emotional triggers so that post-traumatic flashbacks are lessened. You can also rewrite the patterns of your relationships by seeing and feeling yourself having a healthy and happy childhood.

Doreen: As I mentioned in the Introduction, I was a psychotherapist prior to my life-changing brush with death in 1995, when angels warned and protected me during an armed carjacking. While I was a psychotherapist, I was often guided to help women who had father wounds by reimagining their childhoods with better outcomes. We'd visualize fathers apologizing, getting sober, and behaving appropriately. While my clients were consciously aware that they were conjuring a happier movie of their lives, they also realized that they could heal *even if their father never changed or apologized for his actions.*

If visualizing doesn't come easily to you, try writing and reciting a new script for yourself. You can either go back into your past and replay the events as a wise, empowered child, or reimagine your present in an empowered way.

Writing a new script for yourself is powerful. Your brain doesn't know the difference between playacting and real-life events. Practicing handling various scenarios in your mind creates and strengthens new pathways in your brain.

This method is for the purpose of self-healing, and doesn't mean that your relationship with your abuser will be healed. We're not suggesting that you spend time with someone who deeply wounded you, unless you're able to do so without feeling like you're betraying yourself.

Hero Role-Playing

If the idea of rewriting the past doesn't work for you, seeing yourself as the superhero in your own life story can help you overcome the adversity that you may have experienced.

In the play *King Lear*, the king was influenced by Cordelia's sisters, and she felt ostracized. Eventually her father realized that Cordelia was being honest and loyal.

Have you ever felt that way? Misunderstood and perhaps as if your siblings are almost conspiring against you? The Bible is filled with stories like this, as family dysfunction seems to be a part of the human condition. If you have felt like a victim within your own family structure, finding your inner hero can be helpful.

So who are your feminine superheroes? Is it Wonder Woman, Xena, Supergirl, or another character from a fantasy novel you may have read?

If you are a male and feeling disempowered, who are your male superheroes? Perhaps Superman, Batman, or Thor?

Remember, if you choose to identify with your favorite super-hero, to take the *positive* attributes from them. We want to borrow or embody their strength and their capacity to overcome obstacles to conquer their "demons." Of course, that doesn't mean resorting to violence or becoming overly masculine if you are female.

It does mean finding that "inner grit" or determination of saying:

- "I am bigger than my wounds."
- "My inner strength, courage, and faith can overcome."
- "I can outgrow the limitations of the wounded inner child."
- "I can live the life of my dreams."
- "I can easily avoid difficult people, surmount obstacles, and fulfill my own needs."

Resourcing Your Inner Child and Introducing the Magical Child

If you find that doing role-playing with your inner child is too challenging, it may be that either you or your inner child feels under-resourced or not strong enough to be able to face what occurred in your childhood.

Resourcing, a part of play therapy that can be effective for grown-ups too, is a way to see yourself and your inner child in a new light.

It may be time to ask your inner child what will help them feel safer and less frightened. Imagery associated with childhood heroes or heroines you might have had could make your child feel empowered. Did you ever dress up as Supergirl or Wonder Woman, Harry Potter or Spider-Man, or other female or male role models? It may help to actually put on a costume cape or hold a magic-wand prop and pretend to be a powerful child wizard who can direct their own destiny. Or put on metal cuff bracelets and pretend that you're Wonder Woman, directing the universal energy for justice. Or perhaps just visualize a symbolic shield and sword, similar to the ones that Archangel Michael carries, to represent strength.

That wounded or scared part of you may relish this exercise, as your inner child feels free for the first time in your life. You can run around, vanquish demons or other any other negative forces or fears, and feel powerful again.

It may sound silly, but dressing in costume and role-playing can be a powerful way of accessing aspects of yourself that you've never been able to before. You can purchase inexpensive costumes, wands, and accessories at party shops and from online stores, or make your own.

You may find that you have a powerful magical or mystical inner child within you. This magical inner child can make friends with the wounded inner child. Discovering the magical inner child can help you to find magic within yourself and within life again.

Your wounded self has been running your life for way too long, and it is time for your wounded inner child to receive some help from the magical child within you.

The magical child has an amazing imagination, able to devise ways to defeat scary monsters and overcome fearful thinking effortlessly. That part of you knows that you're one with the creative power of the universe and can transform any difficult situation in your life by creating a new, wondrous, exciting one.

REFRAMING YOUR LIFE STORY

Sometimes it can feel like you have no control over what happens to you, or how you feel and react. But you *can* change the story of your life. Up to now, your life may have been filled with a series of losses, painful relationships, and perhaps an underlying feeling of emptiness. That's why it's helpful to rewrite the story you have told about yourself. Instead of seeing yourself as a victim to others, you can choose to see yourself as the triumphant heroine or hero of your story.

Andrew: I have felt a victim of some of the circumstances in my life. I have felt as though some of the feelings of sadness and depression, fear, and anxiety were almost insidious, creeping into my life and my mind, without my doing anything consciously.

I discovered that if you don't take responsibility for how you feel, your life is unlikely to change for the better. You're not responsible for the abuse and abandonment that you've experienced, but you *are* responsible for how you emotionally deal with it from now on. You can allow your painful past to ruin your future, or you can choose for it to make you stronger.

In the past, I had fantasized about meeting a partner who would take away my sadness and loneliness. For a while, I actually did meet someone who did that. What happened, of course, is that the fantasy didn't last. Yet that experience taught me that love isn't found externally. Sure, a healthy relationship can open your heart to love—but it's still *you* doing the heart opening for yourself.

If you don't take responsibility for how you feel, your life is unlikely to change for the better. You're not responsible for the abuse and abandonment that you've experienced, but you are responsible for how you emotionally deal with it from now on. You can allow your painful past to ruin your future, or you can choose for it to make you stronger.

Similar to rewriting your childhood, reframing your story means imagining a happier ending to each *future* experience. Perhaps you imagine yourself successfully standing up to your father, for example. Even if you never do this in real life, the point is to see yourself as the heroine or hero of the story. Use all of your senses to imagine this ending.

Changing your story can help you break the pattern of allowing abusive and abandoning people into your life. Your standards will be raised, and you will expect and only accept people who treat you with the respect that we all deserve. Otherwise, you may forever be looking outside yourself for the solutions, dreaming of the friend or the wonderful partner who is going to rescue you like a knight in shining armor!

We recommend that you don't imagine someone else rescuing you. See yourself rescuing yourself! Or see God, Jesus, Mother Mary, and your guardian angels rescuing you. We *don't* recommend that you imagine anything vengeful, as revenge is never a happy energy. Use all of your senses in this rewriting imagination. Feel, see, hear, and believe that the new happier ending is real.

Your brain and body respond to what you think and how you feel about situations. So you can rewire your brain's routing and help to heal post-traumatic thinking patterns with this method.

Reframing the story of your life can be like trying on a new pair of shoes: uncomfortable at first. Especially if you're accustomed to feeling sorry for yourself. Some people receive so much sympathy and attention for their plight that they're reluctant to be seen as self-sufficient.

You can rewrite the story of your life with you feeling worthy (of love, success, happiness, respect). If your father criticized you or you felt unwanted, then unworthiness can be a lifelong issue unless you take steps to address it.

Some steps to reframe this story include:

- Encourage and support the inner child. Give them the praise that you needed to hear a long time ago: "You can do it," and "You are worthy and loved."

- Place a picture of someone who you feel has self-worth on your vision board or somewhere you will see it every day. It could be a superhero or someone you admire who has achieved a lot. Imagine how they would see themselves and how they would handle criticism. You can superimpose a picture of your face over the other person's.

- Visualize a blue-violet light erasing your negative history. In the past, we would have said that this is like erasing a tape. In this current time, it can be like pressing "Ctrl+Alt+Delete" or erasing files you no longer want on your computer. Imagine the files in your mind called "Unworthy" or "Defective" are all being placed in the trash. Remember to then empty out the trash folder too. After you erase these negative beliefs, it's important to fill the space with new positive beliefs. Prayer and affirmations can rewrite your self-assessment in a loving light.

- Write the words *Worthy, Deserving,* and *High Self-esteem* on pieces of paper and attach them to the back of a chair. Sit in that chair and begin to speak as a person with high self-esteem would speak. Imagine yourself talking to your father in an assertive, self-assured way. Like role-playing, this can be a powerful way to break old patterns of low self-worth. This is great practice if you find spending time with your father to be difficult. You will be prepared and better able to manage this situation when you see him.

Our intention in writing this book has been to help you see yourself as the hero or heroine and the loving nurturer of your own life story. Although this may be hard from your current vantage point, visualizing yourself and your life from the relative distance and comfort of a cinema-like room, you can be kinder and more compassionate toward yourself. And maybe you can even have compassion toward your father for behaving insanely or unlovingly toward you.

FINDING YOUR TRIBE OR SPIRITUAL FAMILY

If you found that your family of origin was painful and your relationship with them seems irreparable, as part of your reparenting process, you can form a type of surrogate family with close friends who are like-minded and supportive.

Andrew: In my 20s, I was in a way adopted by another family. This brought me much healing. I also found enjoyment and had my emotional needs fulfilled through activities such as hiking, yoga, and meditation groups. You may meet your tribe there.

Finding like-minded people on the social networking site Meetup.com can be empowering and will meet your social needs as well. This site lists groups that meet in your area, so that you can make real friends with common interests. I finally joined a Meetup group for writers. We socialized over coffee afterward. I felt relief and a sense of camaraderie. Common interests are a great basis for future friendships or connections. Meetup has practically every type of group imaginable, and the site helps you to create your own group if you'd like.

Doreen: Join a social group or a class based upon your hobbies or interests. When I joined a belly-dance class, I remember feeling intimidated the first time I went, but I quickly relaxed when I realized that all the other women were nervous as well. We all bonded over our shared experience and had so much fun dancing in sparkly outfits to the beautiful music. And one of the women from that class continues to be my dear, close friend.

Many people are longing for times in the past when we lived in tight-knit communities. Some people are acting upon this desire and living in "intentional communities." These communities are composed of like-minded people who choose to live near each other for shared purposes such as tending to an organic garden, cooking and cleaning for each other, and living "off the grid" with solar power and other ecological considerations. These are not like the 1970s communes that encouraged sexual intermingling. Intentional communities are modern ways to develop a "family of choice," especially if your birth family doesn't share your values.

❀ ❀ ❀

Sometimes, you may feel as if you have used most of these strategies, and you have sought counseling and taken steps to address anxiety and depression, and you may despair that nothing seems to be working. You may feel like giving up. If you feel this way, then it actually means that you are on the brink of a breakthrough. It means that you're ready to surrender to God's Divine healing love. In Part III, we will discuss how opening your heart to spiritual healing can help you to fill the hole in your soul left by your father wound and allow you to find meaning in, and ultimately transcend, your suffering.

❀ ❀ ❀ ❀ ❀

PART III

SPIRITUAL TRANSCENDENCE

Chapter Twelve

DIVINE LOVE:
Healing Your Heart Spiritually

In this section, we will discuss spiritual principles that go beyond logic and the intellect. They can bring a sense of deep peace and refreshing calmness, helping to heal that "hole in the soul" that people talk about and that you may have felt yourself.

God isn't something outside of you—you are one with the unlimited and infinite wisdom and love of your Creator. There is no part of you where God is not, as your Creator is omnipresent (meaning "everywhere").

That sense of connection with a Higher Power can also heal insecurities and fears about being alone. It is great to have family, friends, and pets in the physical world. Yet calling upon the Divine can help you feel less needy and more connected, even when no one is physically there for you.

From this thought can come profound feelings of freedom as you realize you're no longer bound by a need for someone else to compensate for the father wound. You realize that you don't have unhealthy dependency on others. When you meet people, you appear more attractive to them, as they feel energy coming toward them from a sense of wholeness, not neediness.

Accept God as your real Father, and your true Creator. As an ideal Father Who has always loved, protected, and cared for you. As a Father Who understands, appreciates, and accepts you. As a Father Who sees you as Divinely perfect, in spiritual truth.

ACCESSING THE DIVINE FATHER

How are you feeling about the concept of a Heavenly Father? If you grew up in mainstream religion and were hurt or offended by people in the church or were taught that God is wrathful and punishing, then you may struggle with this idea. However, it may be an important step in healing your relationship with masculine energy in general.

Making peace with this archetype or energy can be of benefit. Believing in God doesn't mean that you must be religious or follow the protocol of churches or temples. God is part of who you are, as you are one with your Creator. God is your life-force energy and your higher wisdom.

You may not believe in God after your prayers seem to have gone unanswered. You may wonder why God didn't prevent your father from abusing or abandoning you. You may have concluded: *If there is a loving God, why would He allow such suffering?*

While we don't have all of the answers for this relevant question, we can say that God respects everyone's freewill choices— and that includes people who are making choices that hurt other people.

We are certain that God and the angels attempted to steer your father's actions toward responsible parenting. Yet your father didn't hear them. Perhaps he felt unworthy of Divine guidance, or he was an atheist, or so intoxicated or mentally ill that his intuition was shut down. Perhaps he was raised by an abusive or abandoning father, and that's all he knows.

This is not to justify abuse, which is never justifiable. It's to help you wrap your head around how a grown man could have behaved like your father did.

Let's take a moment, breathe, and hold the intention of forgiving God for seemingly not answering your prayers. Let's break through any barriers you erected because you didn't like the people or beliefs of organized religions. Let's heal negative beliefs about men.

When you have a personal relationship with your true Father, God, there's no guilt or fear. There's only compassion and unconditional love. Yes, God may motivate you to make healthy changes or to take positive action. But there is no sense of intimidation or threat in God's guidance. It's all strength and gentleness simultaneously. You can feel God's presence whenever you pray, and however you pray.

In reality, masculine energy is neutral. Healthy masculine energy is a driving and protective force that can help you to achieve and manifest. It's an energy that helps to bring your creative ideas into reality.

SPIRITUALITY AND RELIGION

You can overcome loneliness and heal through spirituality and religion. While overlapping, these two areas also are different:

- *Spirituality* refers to your spiritual beliefs and practices.

- *Religion* refers to an organization that you identify with and/or where you attend services.

Both spirituality and religion are ways to transcend and find meaning in earthly human suffering. They can connect you with God, as a Higher Power from Whom you can draw strength. Sometimes people with father wounds prefer to see the Creator as a gender-neutral or feminine energy. This is fine, as long as the preference is coming from love and attraction instead of unhealed disdain for male energies.

Spirituality is your personal and private connection with the Divine. All of your experiences have shaped your beliefs, so you likely don't fit into any one spiritual or religious "category." Plus, you realize there's no need to label yourself with one type of religious identity.

Yet you may feel called to join a spiritual or religious community of like-minded people. Churches, temples, and spiritual centers are wonderful places to meet new friends and learn new information and skills. Some even offer the opportunity for charitable outreach, which enhances your healthy sense of giving back and helping others. Working in a team within charities or your spiritual/religious organization lends that sense of belonging that we all crave—especially those who didn't receive approval while growing up.

Doreen: I grew up attending Sunday school, and I still love to attend church each weekend. Although I read the Bible daily, and pray and talk with God and Jesus frequently at home, I also like to join with others in joyful worship and song. If you can find the right church, temple, or spiritual center for yourself, you'll make lifelong true friends. Many people meet their spouses in these settings, since it is easier to be in a relationship with a partner who holds similar values.

One way to find a religious path that mirrors your values is to take the online quiz called "What religion am I?" It's posted under different names on various websites, and it consists of answering 20 questions about your beliefs and then receiving an instant online answer as a pop-up (not as an e-mail). I found the quiz to be incredibly accurate.

Whatever the form of worship—whether you attend services, e study, workshops, or prayer circles—we find that those who a belief in a Higher Power lead happier and healthier lives. s show that having a spiritual or religious faith insulates m life stress. Plus, research finds that having a spiritual support community is correlated with better health and longer life expectancy.

If you've had negative experiences with religion, it's understandable why you may have distanced yourself from church or temple. Yet, distancing yourself from God only leads to feelings of emptiness, loneliness, and confusion. It's like being an airplane pilot without contact with the air-traffic controllers.

We all need God's guidance to navigate life! If the male identification of calling God "Father" or "He" upset you, then use alternatives such as "Mother-Father God" or the gender-neutral term "Creator."

※ ※ ※

Remember that religions are people's way of trying to interpret the mysteries of earth life and afterlife. The Bible and other sacred texts offer guidance, yet there's no better Source for guidance than direct communication with your Creator.

To develop a personal relationship with God, create a quiet space to sit or lie down comfortably. God does not require formality, just sincerity. There's no one "right way" to connect with God, so please follow your heart in this experience.

For example, hold the intention of talking with God. This could be during a crisis or a calmer time. Think, write, or speak about your feelings, including feelings that are painful for you to admit. The more real and honest you are with God, the more that you will experience Divine support. Your vulnerability doesn't mean anything negative about you, as every human shares these similar feelings.

Admit everything to God as you would to a trusted best friend. If you have doubts, anger, frustrations, or fears, talk about them too. Pour out your heart about *everything*, and then ask for help.

Your conversation is heard as a prayer, and since all of Heaven respects your freewill choices, you will receive help immediately. The assistance will first come in the form of peaceful energy. You will get a sense that everything will be all right.

Next, you'll receive intuitive messages asking you to take positive action. For example, you may be guided to go to a specific place, or to connect with a certain person, or change your diet or lifestyle in a healthier direction. Like an air-traffic controller, God can see what's around you in every direction.

Sometimes your inner child with father wounds will rebel and resist following Divine guidance, because they don't like being told what to do. If this sounds like you, please talk with God about your resistances, and ask for help in lowering your defenses.

Your relationship with God deepens the more that you have these conversations. As you receive Heavenly help, you begin to trust in your Creator's pure love. You see that God is not an angry, punishing Father, but an unconditionally loving and caring Father.

It may also help to have a similar conversation with Mother Mary, who brings forth the universal, ideal mother energy. Mother Mary can help you to heal concurrent mother wounds, and restore your connection with both the Divine Feminine and Masculine energies.

Finding peace within yourself is the intention. Our society teaches us to be outwardly focused and to work on external goals continuously. Finding that well of peace within you or simply learning how to calm and soothe your emotions is the perfect antidote to life stress.

FOCUSING ON LOVE

Most likely, you're already familiar with concepts of loving the self, positive affirmations, and generally shifting your thoughts toward joy.

One of the real keys to healing is accessing the energy and experience of love. Gratitude is one form that opens your heart and helps you to see the good in yourself and in life.

You may be thinking, *How can this help me to heal?* The answer is that love is a sacred and mystical force that heals you in miraculous ways.

Neuroscience reveals how changing your thoughts can actually change your brain, activating different areas. The brain is an amazing creation.

And your thoughts can change automatically through awakening loving feelings within yourself.

Here are some ways that you can open yourself to love:

- Pray and commune with God, Jesus, Mother Mary, and your guardian angels.

- Feel grateful for what you have in your life and recognize how life does support you and your healing journey.

- Spend time with your pets to help heal your heart. Animals radiate unconditional love and acceptance.

- Give yourself a hug and say "I love you" to yourself.

All of these actions heal by focusing simply on love. By performing them, you are inviting love into your heart. Once love enters your heart, it does all of the healing work for you.

A prayer for healing love:

"Dear God, please help me to accept Your pure and unconditional healing love. Please help me to feel safe in opening my heart to Your trustworthy guidance, and to care about myself enough to allow myself to be loved and loving. Please help me to feel healed."

Invoking Archangel Michael

If you've been emotionally hurt from your relationship with your father, you may distrust men. You may have built a wall that pushes away men who try to get too close to you. And you may be attracted to men who will hurt you, so there's a self-fulfilling prophecy associated with fear of getting hurt.

Archangel Michael, who is an unlimited, tireless, egoless, and nondenominational angel, can help you to safely open your heart to love. He is a peaceful warrior who ensures that only loving people will be with you. If an untrustworthy person attempts to draw near you, Archangel Michael will do one of two things:

- Give you strong intuitive signals to keep away.
- Send them away, so that the person will disappear from your life.

Archangel Michael works with everyone who asks. You never need to worry that you are bothering or tiring the angel, because he is omnipresent, just like God. Besides, the angels don't have physical bodies. They are energy, and energy never tires. Archangel Michael can be with every person simultaneously, having a unique and individual experience with all.

We don't pray to or worship angels (nor do they want to be worshipped). All glory goes to God, Who created angels as guides and protectors for our earthly journeys.

To call upon Archangel Michael, simply say his name and he is instantly there. Here's an invocation that we prefer:

"Archangel Michael, I ask that you stay by my side at this moment and forever. I give you my freewill permission to protect me from those who do not have my best interests at heart. Please help me to choose relationships with loving and trustworthy people."

AWAKENING YOUR SACRED HEART OR THE SACRED SELF

Love is the doorway to connecting with the Divine within you and the Divine expressed through God, Jesus, and the angels.

You may have closed down your heart because it feels safer. You were born a naturally loving and joyful person. You may feel, though, that life has crushed your spirit. Shutting down was a protection mechanism that you used as a way of surviving what may have been a challenging childhood and adolescence or adulthood. You may have had some painful experiences within your relationships that could have compounded your hurt feelings.

The problem with this protective device of shutting down your heart is that it can become a cage. You may feel like you are locked within it.

Fortunately, you have the key to unlock the door and fly free! Having your heart open will lead to healing and transformation.

Exercise for Opening Your Heart

Find a quiet space where you will be undisturbed. Lighting a candle and diffusing some rose oil can assist with the process, but these things are not essential.

Start with deep breaths to help to calm yourself down.

Bring your attention within you, and imagine a locked gate, with heavy doors barring your heart, now opening. Even if the gate opens partially, that is a good start. The gate will open wider as you relax and trust yourself more.

Imagine that beloved Jesus is next to you. You can feel His pure love and compassion for all that you've been through. He empathizes with your painful experiences, and offers you the healing gift of forgiveness.

Allow yourself to see or feel the rays of golden healing light shining from Jesus's heart, to your heart. As you inhale, you may feel the warmth of His love helping you to heal and open your heart.

Stay in this place of love and safety for as long as you feel comfortable.

Both of us have felt deep healings from connecting with Jesus as a present-moment spiritual being, without fear or guilt. His words in the Gospels are very applicable to those of us who are tired of having father wounds burden us: "Come to me, all of you who are tired from carrying heavy loads, and I will give you rest" (Matthew 11:28). We all can connect with Jesus as a conduit of powerful healing simply by asking for His help. We pray that you will be open to doing so.

Chapter Thirteen

❁ ❁ ❁ ❁ ❁

FINDING PEACE:
Life Lesson Integration

We believe that God has a Divine order and plan for all of us, and that we come to Earth to learn some very heavy-duty lessons that ultimately allow us to grow spiritually. All the while, God is helping us: "He heals the broken-hearted and bandages their wounds" (Psalm 147:3).

Careful planning occurs with every lifetime. Each life is precious and offers opportunities for spiritual growth. Your social standing, family background, and cultural background have all been carefully chosen by God prior to your incarnating into this life.

This likely means that your soul carefully chose your father as well. That can be difficult to accept or believe; however, take a little time to consider what might be your soul's motivation in choosing your father in this life.

Some possible explanations could be that you came to learn forgiveness and compassion that needed to occur together. Perhaps your soul volunteered to be an earth angel to a dysfunctional family. So you incarnated as a sweet child in a harsh household and never felt like you fit into that family. You *didn't*. Bringing the peace and forgiveness of God to a family in need was your Divine assignment.

The lower energies of darkness often "use" people so that fear and chaos can spread. Your father may have been susceptible to this type of possession because of substance abuse or his own disconnection from God. Perhaps the darkness was trying to thwart your beautiful life purpose by controlling your father's actions.

This is not to absolve him of his responsibilities, as every person has the choice to follow either God or the ego. However, this might be a reason for you to increase your prayers for spiritual protection for yourself and your family. This knowledge may also allow you to overcome fears of moving forward with your life purpose.

HEALING FATHER WOUNDS AFTER HE'S PASSED AWAY

What if your father has passed away? Is there any possibility of healing your relationship with him while you are still on Earth? The answer is *yes*!

A woman named Barbara felt guilty because she'd taken her father to an assisted living center, and his health had deteriorated. She was angry with herself for not visiting him more frequently, because she was so busy with work and her children. And when she was honest with herself, Barbara realized that she didn't want to see her father. "He was so unpleasant!" she recalled.

When her father slipped into a coma, Barbara as the only child was given the unfortunate task of signing the papers to take him off life support. As Barbara watched her father take his last breath, she struggled with grief over her life-and-death decision. She also mourned the death of the fantasy that her father would open his eyes and say something loving to her. She realized that she'd never have the ideal father love that she'd always craved.

Barbara was able to heal her feelings by meeting with her church pastor, who gave her encouragement and prayerful support. Her pastor officiated the funeral, and the church members made sure that Barbara was surrounded by people who loved her. The support gave Barbara hope that she was lovable, not the bad person her guilt had spoken about.

Since her father's passing, Barbara sees butterflies all the time. She feels it's a Heavenly sign that her father is grateful for her daughterly support, and that he's sorry for not being the father she needed. Each time she sees a butterfly, Barbara says, "Hi, Dad," and she feels herself lighten up as the butterfly flies skyward.

The truth is that after your father passes over, he may feel remorse and pain as a result of realizing the impact of his actions when he was alive.

We believe that we all undergo a compassionate life review after we pass. Our actions, omissions, and intentions will be examined in a compassionate way. When we realize that we've hurt others and we see the impact of our actions on the life of that person, we may try to rectify and fix the damage we've done. Angels may visit the person we've hurt and extend our apologies, or help them to have a better life.

If you have unresolved emotions with your father, this may be difficult to fathom. In truth, if your father has passed over, he is probably feeling remorseful and craving your forgiveness. Having a belief and a trust that there is a Divine justice can bring you peace of mind. People do have to face themselves in this life and in the afterlife. They are made aware of what pain they caused you and often suffer when they realize the damage they did.

Some abuse survivors have told us that they are happy their father is suffering in purgatory, and that it serves him right after he made his children suffer. The adult children don't want to forgive the father, because they believe his actions were unforgivable. Yet when we store such rage within ourselves, we are the ones who suffer, not the abuser. And our own children don't receive the benefit of our fully opened and loving heart if a part of us is obsessed with revenge.

SOUL GROWTH THROUGH FORGIVENESS

True forgiveness means having compassion for those who are insane enough to abuse or abandon a child. Forgiving your father helps your soul to grow, opening the door to higher spiritual dimensions, and is the only true path to inner peace. You never need to forgive his actions, but you do need to detox yourself of old, stored toxic anger. It's a tall order, but remember that you have Jesus and lots of angels to help you with this healing work.

You can purchase a special "God box" online by searching for "God box" or "prayer box," or you can use a simple cardboard shoe box that you decorate with images of angels and flowers and write the word *God* on. You may also designate a sacred space in your home for an altar, where you can place your God box and pictures of Jesus, Mother Mary, or archangels that you connect with. Prayer requests and intentions for healing yourself and others can be placed in the God box. It is a symbolic way of "letting go and letting God."

An alternative to burning a letter to your father is to place it on your altar for a while. Ask God, Jesus, and the angels to heal your relationship with the father figure who hurt you. You can dispose of the letter after you feel that the healing has occurred. You will know you have healed when you can wish your father well. You may find yourself praying for him and asking God to bless him too.

You may feel victimized and ask, "Why do I have to be the one to forgive, when he was the one who abused me?" It can feel like you're the only one putting work into healing the relationship. And that may be true if he's incapable (because of emotional damage, intoxication, lower-energy possession, or mental health issues) of compassion toward others.

Remember, though, that forgiveness is for *your* soul, not to change *him*. Forgiveness is not the same as justifying or overlooking someone's behavior.

For a woman named Ariel, the suicidal death of her father was a turning point in her life and a trigger for her to commence a spiritual path.

Ariel consulted a spiritual counselor who helped her choose the path of forgiveness. She felt a burden lift from her shoulders and instant relief! Later Ariel turned to spirituality as her career as well. Today, Ariel feels that she has healed her inner child and found peace with her father.

The cycle of pain can continue until we decide to stop it. No one said it was going to be easy, being here on Earth during this tumultuous time of change on the planet, but it *is* possible.

HEALING YOUR VULNERABILITY

If you have lingering feelings of unworthiness, the first step is to be aware of them and have compassion for yourself. Many of us have persistent feelings of not measuring up, no matter what level of success we may achieve.

You may have already realized that father wounds can lead to these feelings of unworthiness and powerlessness. They are a *symptom* of father wounds, not a statement of who you are. In spiritual truth, you were made in the image and likeness of God. God is worthy, and therefore so are you! God is powerful, and therefore so are you! God is your true Father, and God loves you!

The spiritual truth of who you are is whole and perfect. God doesn't make mistakes. Please don't see yourself as damaged or perpetually wounded. Please don't make your abused past your primary identity. Yes, as a human you experience suffering, yet that is not the spiritual truth of who you are.

Discover the vast being that you really are. If you focus only upon your pain, you are seeing but a small reflection of your experience. Meditation, spending time in nature, and creative activities can help you to discover other facets of who you are.

Andrew: For a long time, I saw myself as powerless and was caught up in victim mentality—feeling bullied and unfairly treated, and finding myself in one-sided relationships. I resigned myself that such was my lot in life. I am a little embarrassed to admit that I have felt this way, even while walking a spiritual path. Although I was a Divine being who had gifts, talents, and abilities, I could not control how people responded to me. No one can.

Here is a meditation that helped me learn how to love and value myself, and that hopefully can help you as well:

Meditation for Filling Yourself from the Well of Compassion within You

Take a few deep breaths and calm your breathing down. Notice the thoughts that come in and out of your consciousness and just let them go. Don't push against them—simply accept and allow.

Focus your attention within your heart space and your belly and notice how those areas feel. Let go of any tension or worry you may be carrying; simply notice it and choose peace and tranquility instead.

Deep inside you is a flame, light, or inner beacon that you can see or sense. That Divine flicker can become brighter and brighter until you feel it enveloping your entire body.

Allow whatever figure that symbolizes compassion come to you, such as your guardian angel, Mother Mary, or Jesus; you can call on them to be with you. They hold your hand, and they place their other hand on your heart.

Feel any remaining pain, worry, or hurt melt away from this Divine heat.

Say the words "Compassion . . . I am deeply compassionate . . . My compassion envelops me and those around me . . . It is safe for me to let go of defenses . . . I know that the universe is perfectly balanced, and I surrender to Divine justice to right wrongs."

Feel the weight on your shoulders lifting. Know that throughout your life, you've done the best you could. Be willing to forgive yourself for what you think you've done or not done.

Allow the healing salve of compassion to melt away any of the hurt that you may be feeling.

Chapter Fourteen

❈ ❈ ❈ ❈ ❈

WISDOM GAINED FROM FATHER WOUNDS

It is very easy to be caught up in the pain of your past. Anger, and wanting to right the wrongs from your childhood and adolescence, is a natural response. Hopefully, reading this book has helped you work through the feelings of hurt and betrayal. Now you might be ready to consider what you've learned from your experiences with your father.

- Can you think of any life lessons you've gained as a result of your father wounds?

- Have you noticed that your suffering led you to find your spiritual path?

- Would it be safe to say that your experiences have made you who you are today? And that you've learned how to survive and be strong?

If you have survived the experience and have chosen to face your own pain and work toward forgiveness, it is likely that you feel compassion for others' suffering. For many people, trying to derive meaning from their pain can be a doorway to spiritual awareness.

When you're ready, the teachers present themselves. As you have chosen to take steps toward healing your father wounds, you will likely attract teachers, therapists, and other people who have gone through similar experiences to your own and bring healing modalities designed to help those in your situation.

There is a Divine symphony to all of this. You will start to make connections. The law of attraction is one way of explaining this. As you hold the intention to heal, you draw to you all the help you need.

You will begin to feel a sense of "rightness" and that you are being looked after somehow. All of this is true. Beneath the surface of this amazing life on Earth, an invisible team, guides, and helpers behind the scenes work hard to deliver us to awareness.

If you can come to real peace with your experiences with your father, then you have earned the equivalent of a Ph.D. in spiritual growth.

SPIRITUAL-GROWTH LESSONS

In truth, dealing with father wounds is a part of your life purpose. If you heal this area of your life, other areas will benefit, and you can use the lessons you've learned to help others.

Yet we're all works in progress. Some days, you may feel that you have it all together with your father. Then something may trigger you, and you instantly regress to the hurt inner child. Once again, like peeling the layers of the onion, please keep going.

Patience with Yourself and with Life

Reading this book shows that you are sincere about self-development and self-healing work, particularly on issues relating to father wounds.

Naturally, this can take time to resolve. It does become easier. You come to know yourself better, and you can see the recurring patterns in your relationships and work environment.

If you have repeatedly found yourself in the same types of relationships as a way of trying to compensate for your father wound, please be extra gentle and compassionate with yourself. You always learn something new. It can feel like a merry-go-round; however, our development is more of a spiral, approaching ever closer to wholeness and healing. Each time you repeat a pattern, you can see more clearly why you are doing this again and which aspect of yourself is driving your experience.

Discernment to Choose Healthy Relationships: Awareness of Red Flags to Guide You

If you've been attracted to older men who are financially stable, emotionally unavailable men, or alpha males who control everyone and everything, this is a sign of looking for a father substitute. Unconsciously, there's a desire to win your father's love through a man who reminds you of him. You do everything to please this man, but like your father, his heart is closed and he can't give or receive love.

The reasons why you may be attracted to unhealthy relationships can be complex. Father issues are just one significant reason. By committing to understanding the recurring patterns, you've taken the important first step to enact a change in your situation.

Once you have recognized your patterns clearly with a lot of self-reflection, you can see the red flags much more easily, and you can choose to not repeat the same patterns again and again.

If you're able to recognize unhealthy patterns and red flags warning you away from dysfunctional relationships, you can save yourself a lot of time, energy, and heartache. It's better to be alone than to begin another unhealthy relationship. By healing your father wound, you can learn to make wise choices in relationships after being on the merry-go-round of unhealthy connections.

That includes having the strength and self-love to stay away from ex-lovers who you know are wrong for you. Prayer can give you the strength to say "No" to dysfunctional relationships and "Yes" to enjoying a life of true love.

Empathy and Helping Others

If you've suffered due to having an unhappy relationship with your father, you may not realize until later that this wound has taught you a lot. As you are on this healing journey, you have the potential—and you might already have the desire—to help others who may be in a similar situation.

These painful events may have meant that you've developed deeper insights into why people are the way they are. This, in turn, can give you compassion for human suffering and why we tend to repeat patterns unless we bring them to Divine light and choose to heal them.

Although everyone develops in different ways and you cannot force others to accept your wisdom, your experiences can equip you with the empathy and life skills to become a professional helper (a counselor, for example, or a social worker, pastor, or psychologist) and/or an intuitive healer (such as an oracle card reader or energy healer). You will be an amazing counselor, because you've addressed a key life issue.

There is a concept in psychology known as the "wounded healer." Many people (including the two of us) have experienced pain and suffering within their own family and relationships that have spurred them on a spiritual path.

Healers don't need to be completely healed themselves. In fact, it's virtually impossible to be 100 percent mentally and emotionally healthy. If healers waited until their lives were "fixed" before beginning their healing work, there would *be* no healers.

The key isn't whether you *have* issues; it's whether you're *aware* of them. Know that your healing work may trigger memories of your own issues. Pray and do your best not to project your "stuff" onto your client. Training with an experienced healer can also help you to avoid projection of this kind.

Andrew: I chose social work as a career because I can understand and relate to others who are going through difficult times.

Had I had a happy childhood and a healthy relationship with my stepfather and birth father, it's unlikely that I would have chosen such a challenging—but rewarding—profession as social work . . . and I wouldn't be writing this book.

As a result of the suffering you may have experienced as a child, your brain may be rewired to be sensitized to conflict, and you may absorb other people's emotions. Of course, not everyone is supersensitive; however, there is usually one member of a family who is. I can definitely say that *I* was that one in my family. My sisters dealt with the pain of our upbringing in different ways.

For me, I found myself compelled to understand *why* my family was the way it is. *Why are the patterns occurring, and how can I change them?* I wondered as a child.

Of course, trying to play "social worker" within your own family probably isn't a great idea, as you're too close to the members to objectively help them. However, with the insights I gained about my own family dynamics, I can help other families through my therapy sessions.

Maybe the hurt *you* experienced as a child has shaped your life in rich and unexpected ways as well. Maybe you can discover there is a destiny and a purpose with all of this.

Being a Free Thinker!

One "hidden blessing" of having a father wound is that you probably think outside the box and you may be a bit of a free spirit. Another way of saying this is that you might be a nonconformist.

Are you a trailblazer? Do you live an unconventional lifestyle? These are wonderful traits because you probably aren't following the same tried-and-true path that your parents followed. You have broken free from the confines of your upbringing. In fact, you may be the one who's destined to break the unhealthy cycles of your forefathers.

It's time for freethinking, unconventional, creative, and innovative people to step forward into positions of leadership and influence. If we all just conformed to what our parents did and lived our lives to please them, we wouldn't be able to fulfill a destiny that breaks the mold.

Doreen: I was not raised with many rules or guidelines. My mother and father, who both suffered at the hands of controlling, angry, alcoholic parents, decided to raise my brother and me with free rein to do whatever we wanted. So I followed my bliss, which sometimes involved situations and relationships that most parents would have warned me against. Yet this also meant that I learned a ton of life lessons early. I learned to take responsibility for my actions and for building my future, instead of blaming others or waiting for them to take the lead.

It's the same with you. In spite of your pain, you've learned to rely upon yourself. You've learned that you can't rely upon other people to approve of you or guide your next step. You've became stronger in your convictions and more independent in your thinking.

Andrew: Growing up with a repressive religious background and a lack of father figures or mentors meant that I had to go out and find my own answers to questions about my life, career, and identity. There are probably areas in which a supportive father would also have provided *you* with guidance. As a result of not having someone to guide you in these areas, you're given the opportunity to discover a life purpose for yourself. From my own experience, in my late teenage years there was an inner push for me to probe some of life's deeper questions.

FORGED IN FIRE: SEEING YOUR STRENGTHS AND FINDING YOUR SPIRITUAL PURPOSE

As a social worker, I (Andrew) discovered that focusing upon someone's strengths and abilities can be an effective way to help them move on from the difficulties they are experiencing.

People who face difficult circumstances can often feel that they are powerless to change them. You may feel almost victimized by the life that you are living. You may also feel as though life is conspiring against you as you face one seemingly doomed relationship after another. You may believe that you're cursed or unlucky, or that only rich and powerful people have enjoyable lives.

Have you ever asked yourself, *What did I ever do to deserve the life that I have?* The reality is that it *isn't* and *wasn't* your fault if your father left, wasn't there for you, or was abusive, and *you have done nothing wrong.*

Have you done the journaling, said the prayers and affirmations, and found that things haven't changed or that you feel that you are banging your head against a brick wall?

There is a concept in social work called *oppression*, where it appears that sets of circumstances, relationships, and cultural factors all seem to coalesce and form a sticky web that we feel caught in.

Freeing yourself is possible and very doable. There are many people who have found themselves in similar oppressive patterns, transcended difficult circumstances, and then gone on to help others.

One of the ways of finding your way out is to focus upon your strengths, gifts, and abilities. Each one of us is born with a purpose. There are certain things that you have come here to learn. Some of the big life lessons involve developing more love, compassion, wisdom, patience, and forgiveness. These are monumental virtues that you come to express in this challenging Earth school. In addition, you have a personal mission or purpose, which can include being a parent and having a fulfilling career helping children or adults, animals, plants, or the ocean.

Focusing upon finding your purpose is the same as focusing upon your strengths and abilities. For example, if you have experienced challenges in your life, seeing yourself as a survivor and even a thriver is one way of doing so.

In other words, view yourself as *resilient*. Even though you've faced difficulties, you're still here. It's as though there's some invisible glue that has held you together, even when your life may have been falling apart.

What is that mystical quality or magic glue that keeps us here and on our path?

For many, it is a spiritual belief system, trusting in God and Jesus, or faith that life gets better. Spirituality is important in helping you to be happy, and in finding a sense of purpose and meaning.

Please consider what some of your strengths are:

"I am _____ [intelligent, wise, resilient, resourceful, compassionate, whole, solution focused, caring, loving, loyal, trustworthy, generous, hardworking, and so on]."

This is the truth of who you are, as a spiritual being having a human experience. There is so much more to who you really are than painful emotions and a sense of feeling victimized.

At the end of your life, you'll be happiest about those moments when you extended love, kindness, and compassion, bringing more light to the world. You won't be at all focused upon the darker moments of your life, except for the healthy ways in which you dealt with them.

Change your internal dialogue, and sincerely compliment yourself and others on your and their strengths. This positive energy helps *them* and *you.*

MOVING ON FROM GRIEF AND
SADNESS AND LIVING A VICTORIOUS LIFE!

You may notice that after you've shed tears, expressed your anger safely, written that letter to your father and burned it, and used any other cathartic processes, such as talking to a friend or counselor, journaling about your feelings, or writing your fears and hurts down and placing them in a God box, your life begins to take on a new tranquility and peace.

Andrew: One of the things I have noticed after my father wounds began healing is that I have experienced more peace and contentment with myself. My pangs of heartache and loneliness dissipated. I attracted several genuine friends, and the less-than-genuine relationships fell by the wayside. I felt so much more at ease with myself, my pain, and my life.

My father wound took its rightful place within the tapestry of my life. In fact, as I reflect upon that thread now, I can see that what was once a gaping tear has transformed into something golden. I believe this is sacred alchemy.

You can see the gifts that a wound innately carries within it. That can mean you have courageously faced those scary feelings. You've been able to shine the light of your awareness on them. Once you face them, they are banished with the help of God, Jesus, Mother Mary, Archangel Michael, and your guardian angels.

※ ※ ※ ※ ※

AFTERWORD

YOUR CONTINUING JOURNEY
WITH FATHER THERAPY

If you have been able to read to the end of the book, well done! We acknowledge that it hasn't been an easy read, and perhaps you've found it confronting and challenging at times.

We wanted to make the book relatable and real. We used our own clinical experiences as a guide to explain the possible impact of father wounds. God will guide you to any additional healing techniques, books, or therapies that you may need to complete this process.

In the meantime, gently remind yourself to be at peace with the process of life. Here are some other reminders we'd like to leave you with.

PLEASE KNOW THAT . . .

— **You are not alone in recognizing and healing your father wounds.** There are thousands of women and men finding their way through this issue. Many others have been able to heal and to move on with their lives.

— **The journey does get easier once you have done some of the heavy lifting.** You *will* have more and more experiences of calm and feeling better about yourself.

If you have experienced significant trauma, it is likely the effects will last a long time. You may experience emotional flashbacks, which are those challenging emotional states of feeling powerless and afraid. You may have feelings of shame, guilt, loneliness, and low mood—sometimes all mixed in simultaneously. These moods can spring up at any old time—sometimes there is a clear trigger; other times there is not. These feelings are just calling out for your loving attention.

Once you gently face and feel them, emotions lose their power. Once you feel confidence in your God-given power, you will be less afraid, and you will experience more calm and more peace with yourself and your life.

— With patience and persistence, you can overcome any unhealthy habits. You can and you will live a more empowered life, with healthy friendships and hobbies, a fulfilling career, and meaningful relationships, over time.

Please be extra gentle and compassionate with yourself during this time of healing. If you're feeling overwhelmed, be sure to ask for and accept qualified human support, such as calling a crisis hotline, attending a 12-step support meeting, talking with a pastoral counselor, or seeing a therapist. Our strong suggestion is only to work with *happy* therapists and teachers, since they can teach happiness because they *are* happy. Please use any of the self-help techniques in this book or any others that you might find helpful.

CHECK IN WITH YOUR INNER CHILD REGULARLY

If you're feeling sad for no particular reason, ask your inner child, "What would you like me to do for you today?"

Often the inner child will say, "I want to have more fun," or "I want to play." That doesn't mean you need to ignore your responsibilities. It can mean that you need to make a promise, and honor that promise, to yourself and your inner child.

Commit to making time for play each day or at least each week. This can involve:

- Playing with your pet or a child

- Swinging on swings or climbing a tree

- Preparing and eating something healthy and enjoyable

- Watching a lighthearted movie

Laughter can release pain. You can actually let go of issues through laughter. Allow tears to flow if they come up. Please don't stifle them.

Unleash your creativity by playing an instrument, drawing, or coloring. Express your inner child's hurt artistically. Draw a picture of how your child is feeling. If that picture is sad, ask your angels, God, and your Higher Self: "What would heal or cheer my child?" or "What attributes or qualities are needed for me to heal?"

You can sprinkle glitter on the drawing, or paste stickers of beautiful flowers or angels surrounding the figure. These actions can be weaving a Divine protective shield so that your inner child will feel safe and loved.

Use colors to represent the qualities your inner child needs to survive and thrive—for example, white light for love, purple for protection, deep green or pink for compassion, and yellow for empowerment.

Dress in sparkly outfits, in bright healing purple, blue, green, or pink, or as your favorite superhero. Wear fairy wings. Throw a fun dress-up party!

COMMIT TO SELF-RESPECT

Lovingly protecting your inner child means that they are no longer throwing tantrums and running the show. All children appreciate loving boundaries and knowing the rules. It actually makes them feel safe. So you can be firm with your inner child.

That also goes for the inner critic that may surface. You can accept that voice; however, you don't need to let it overpower or overwhelm you. Your inner critic may say things like *Aren't you over this wound yet?* or *You will never heal.* Critics always criticize, including the inner critic. Fortunately, you don't need to listen to *any* criticism except for lovingly constructive suggestions that will help you improve your life.

You can chip away at this issue by changing the way you think about yourself. Start to think and *act* like someone who has self-worth:

- **Treat your mind with respect.** That can mean gently noticing the times you put yourself down, even with self-deprecating humor, and choosing again. Explore new ideas and learning opportunities.

- **Choose loving thoughts about yourself.** Affirm that you are good enough and worthy simply because you are a child of God.

- **Design your career to meet your true passions and interests.** This will reinforce your self-worth and give you a sense of purpose and meaning as well.

- **Find a supportive spiritual path that resonates deeply for you.** Develop regular spiritual practices such as meditation and prayer. Study a philosophy that you have always been interested in. Join a spiritual group or start your own, and discuss spiritual writings and philosophies. Start attending church or temple to build your support community and deepen your connection to God.

All of these choices, when made consistently and lovingly, will bring a sense of well-being. With persistence, your thoughts of not feeling good enough will fade and be replaced with the unconditional, pure Divine love that is always within and around you.

❈ ❈ ❈ ❈ ❈

Appendix

Community Resources and Therapy Options

Co-dependency support. If you're in a relationship with an addict, or you chronically people-please or avoid conflict at any cost, you'd benefit from attending the free meetings of Al-Anon. To find a meeting near you or online, please visit Al-Anon.org.

EMDR (Eye Movement Desensitization and Reprocessing). Find a local therapist who is specialized in trauma-release work who can help you to clear the symptoms of trauma from your life. Visit EMDR.com.

Drug and alcohol counseling groups. If you are working through addiction issues, finding a support group such as Alcoholics Anonymous or Narcotics Anonymous can help you. Local community health services also provide counseling and support for individuals and families who are experiencing issues. They can provide information on accessing detox and residential rehabilitation programs as well. Visit AA.org.

Men's groups. Men are now gathering and are able to express their wounds and vulnerability with the support of other men. There are men's personal growth workshops, and anger management workshops that can very helpful for men who are feeling alone and in need of the support and acceptance of other men. Contact your local community mental health center to find a meeting near you, or find a therapist who specializes in men's issues.

Therapists. You can find detailed professional listings for psychologists, psychiatrists, psychotherapists, counselors, support groups, and treatment centers in the United States and Canada at therapists.psychologytoday.com; check out the directory of the American Psychological Association: http://locator.apa.org; or look up the professional organization in your country of residence. It's also helpful to get referrals for local therapists from your physician, your pastor, your 12-step sponsor, or trusted friends.

Women's groups. There are women's groups that deal with self-esteem, assertiveness, and managing emotions that can be helpful and healing. Meeting women who are on a healing journey similar to your own is empowering and liberating. Contact your local community mental health center to find a meeting near you, or look for a therapist who specializes in women's issues.

❧ ❧ ❧ ❧ ❧

BIBLIOGRAPHY

Battaglia, Salvatore. *The Complete Guide to Aromatherapy*. 2nd ed. Brisbane, Australia: International Centre of Holistic Aromatherapy, 2003.

Bradshaw, John. *Homecoming: Reclaiming and Championing Your Inner Child*. New York: Bantam Books, 1990.

Fathers Unite. "Some Statistics on Fatherlessness." Accessed August 2015. http://fathersunite.org/statistics_on_fatherlessnes.html.

Firestone, Robert. "Emotional Hunger vs. Love: Emotional hunger is not love. It is a strong emotional need." February 24, 2009. https://www.psychologytoday.com /blog/the-human-experience/200902/emotional-hunger-vs-love.

Hay, Louise. *You Can Heal Your Life*. Carlsbad, CA: Hay House, 1999.

Keller, Sonja. "If 'Daddy Issues' Are Affecting Your Relationships, Read This." May 30, 2014. http://www.mindbodygreen.com/0-13968/if-daddy-issues-are-affecting -your-relationships-read-this.html.

Kruk, Edward. "Father Absence, Father Deficit, Father Hunger: The Vital Importance of Paternal Presence in Children's Lives." May 23, 2012. http://www.psychologytoday.com/blog/co-parenting-after-divorce/201205 /father-absence-father-deficit-father-hunger.

Kessler, David. "The 5 Stages of Grief." Accessed June 2015. www.grief.com /the-five-stages-of-grief.

Leonard, Linda Schierse. *The Wounded Woman: Healing the Father-Daughter Relationship*. Athens, OH: Swallow Press, 1982.

Matthews, Scott. "Dads Through the Ages: A History." Accessed March 2016. https://www.dad.info/fatherhood/being-dad/dads-through-the-ages-a-history.

Merril, T. "The Shadow Father." Diamonds and Toads Blog. Accessed March 2016. http://www.diamondsandtoads.com/2009/11/shadow-father.html.

Miller, Ali. Instructor's Manual for Salvador Minuchin on Family Therapy. With Salvador Minuchin and Jay Lappin. Mill Valley, CA: Psychotherapy.net, 2011. https://www.psychotherapy.net/data/uploads/5113e45715ce5.pdf.

Myss, Caroline. *Archetype Cards*. Guidebook. Carlsbad, CA: Hay House, 2003.

NYU Langone Medical Center / New York University School of Medicine. "Brain images reveal first physical evidence that AA prayers reduce cravings." *Science-Daily*. May 12, 2016. www.sciencedaily.com/releases/2016/05/160512142925.htm.

Pehanick, Maggie. "11 Great Word of Wisdom from Onscreen Dads—in GIFs!" June 18, 2016. http://www.popsugar.com/entertainment/Best-Movie-Dads-Advice -From-Movie-Dads-8805562#photo-8805562.

Phares, Vicky. *Fathers and Developmental Psychopathology*. New York: John Wiley & Sons, Inc., 1995.

Sawyer, Sarah. "Fairy Tale Fathers and Their Failings." *Sarah* Sawyer (blog). July 15, 2011. http://www.sarahsawyer.com/2011/07/fairy-tale-fathers-and-their -failings.

Sherwood, Patricia. *The Healing Art of Clay Therapy*. Melbourne, Australia: ACER Press, 2004.

Smith, Ann W. *Grandchildren of Alcoholics: Another Generation of Co-Dependency*. Deerfield Beach, FL: Health Communications, Inc., 1988.

Trent, John, and Gary Smalley. *The Blessing: Giving the Gift of Unconditional Love and Acceptance*. Nashville, TN: Thomas Nelson, 2011.

Virtue, Doreen. *Assertiveness for Earth Angels: How to Be Loving Instead of "Too Nice."* Carlsbad, CA: Hay House, 2013.

———. *Don't Let Anything Dull Your Sparkle: How to Break Free of Negativity and Drama*. Carlsbad, CA: Hay House, 2015.

———. *Losing Your Pounds of Pain*. Carlsbad, CA: Hay House, 1993.

Vogt, Gregory Max, and Stephen T. Sirridge. *Like Son, Like Father: Healing the Father-Son Wound in Men's Lives*. New York: Springer US, 1991.

Young, Jeffrey E., and Janet S. Klosko. *Reinventing Your Life: The Breakthrough Program to End Negative Behavior . . . and Feel Great Again*. New York: Plume Books, 1994.

※ ※ ※ ※ ※

ABOUT THE AUTHORS

Doreen Virtue holds three university degrees in counseling psychology. A former psychotherapist specializing in treating eating disorders and addictions, Doreen began focusing upon spiritual counseling following a brush with death and miraculous Divine intervention in 1995. She is the author of over 70 books and card decks, and her work is published in 38 languages worldwide. She has appeared on *Oprah*, CNN, *The View*, the BBC, and countless other media outlets internationally. Doreen writes a weekly column for *Woman's World* magazine, hosts a call-in weekly show on Hay House Radio, and gives workshops via online video courses through HayHouseU.com and EarthAngel.com.

Website: AngelTherapy.com

ANGEL THERAPY®

Andrew Karpenko holds a master of social work degree and has worked within the mental health, drug and alcohol, and management areas since 2001. As a social worker, he has counseled women, men, and children across a broad range of issues.

Andrew blends intuition with his professional skills and knowledge to provide an integrated approach to healing emotional wounds and childhood issues. He has experienced challenges within his own family of origin and has learned to manage and heal from them, and he is passionate about working with people who are ready for change, helping them break away from limiting beliefs and negative patterns and transcend the impact of deep emotional wounds. He conducts counseling sessions by telephone, e-mail, and live video.

Website: Facebook.com/AndrewKarpenkoAuthor

Hay House Titles of Related Interest

YOU CAN HEAL YOUR LIFE, the movie, starring Louise Hay & Friends
(available as a 1-DVD program, an expanded
2-DVD set, and an online streaming video)
Learn more at www.hayhouse.com/louise-movie

THE SHIFT, the movie, starring Dr. Wayne W. Dyer
(available as a 1-DVD program, an expanded
2-DVD set, and an online streaming video)
Learn more at www.hayhouse.com/the-shift-movie

⚜ ⚜ ⚜

ANGER RELEASING;
FORGIVENESS/LOVING THE INNER CHILD; and
HOW TO LOVE YOURSELF (audios), by Louise Hay

CLEAR HOME, CLEAR HEART:
Learn to Clear the Energy of People & Places,
by Jean Haner

HEALING YOUR FAMILY HISTORY:
5 Steps to Break Free of Destructive Patterns,
by Rebecca Linder Hintze

JOINING FORCES: Empowering Male Survivors to Thrive,
by Howard Fradkin, Ph.D.

NO STORM LASTS FOREVER: Transforming Suffering into Insight,
by Dr. Terry A. Gordon

REPETITION: Past Lives, Life, and Rebirth,
by Doris Eliana Cohen, Ph.D.

YOU CAN HEAL YOUR HEART:
Finding Peace After a Breakup, Divorce, or Death,
by Louise Hay and David Kessler

All of the above are available at your local bookstore,
or may be ordered by contacting Hay House (see next page).

⚜ ⚜ ⚜

We hope you enjoyed this Hay House book. If you'd like
to receive our online catalog featuring additional information
on Hay House books and products, or if you'd like to find
out more about the Hay Foundation, please contact:

Hay House, Inc., P.O. Box 5100, Carlsbad, CA 92018-5100
(760) 431-7695 or (800) 654-5126
(760) 431-6948 (fax) or (800) 650-5115 (fax)
www.hayhouse.com® • www.hayfoundation.org

✼ ✼ ✼

Published and distributed in Australia by:
Hay House Australia Pty. Ltd., 18/36 Ralph St., Alexandria NSW 2015
Phone: 612-9669-4299 • *Fax:* 612-9669-4144
www.hayhouse.com.au

Published and distributed in the United Kingdom by:
Hay House UK, Ltd., Astley House, 33 Notting Hill Gate, London W11 3JQ
Phone: 44-20-3675-2450 • *Fax:* 44-20-3675-2451 • www.hayhouse.co.uk

Published and distributed in the Republic of South Africa by:
Hay House SA (Pty), Ltd., P.O. Box 990, Witkoppen 2068
info@hayhouse.co.za • www.hayhouse.co.za

Published in India by:
Hay House Publishers India, Muskaan Complex, Plot No. 3,
B-2, Vasant Kunj, New Delhi 110 070 • *Phone:* 91-11-4176-1620
Fax: 91-11-4176-1630 • www.hayhouse.co.in

Distributed in Canada by:
Raincoast Books, 2440 Viking Way, Richmond, B.C. V6V 1N2
Phone: 1-800-663-5714 • *Fax:* 1-800-565-3770 • www.raincoast.com

✼ ✼ ✼

Access New Knowledge.
Anytime. Anywhere.

Learn and evolve at your own pace with the world's leading experts.

www.hayhouseU.com